PROJECT
MANAGEMENT
FOR
PROFIT

JOE KNIGHT
ROGER THOMAS
AND BRAD ANGUS
WITH JOHN CASE

A FAILSAFE GUIDE
TO KEEPING PROJECTS
ON TRACK AND
ON BUDGET

PROJECT
MANAGEMENT
FOR
PROFIT

HARVARD BUSINESS REVIEW PRESS

Boston, Massachusetts

Library of Congress Cataloging-in-Publication Data

Project management for profit : a failsafe guide to keeping projects on track
and on budget / Joe Knight ... [et al.].
    p. cm.
  ISBN 978-1-4221-4417-6 (alk. paper)
  1. Project management. 2. Cost control. I. Knight, Joe, 1963-
  HD69.P75P72866 2012
  658.4'04–dc23
                          2012012923

The paper used in this publication meets the requirements of the American
National Standard for Permanence of Paper for Publications and Documents
in Libraries and Archives Z39.48-1992.

To my wife, Donielle, and to the seven Js—
Jacob, Jordan, Jewel, Jessica, James, Jonah, and
Joseph Christian (JC).

—J.K.

To my parents, Glenn and Linda, whose years
of nudging and encouragement finally paid off;
to my children, Nick Thomas and Andrea Pitts; and
to my canine children, Greta, Wookie, and Ripley.

—R.T.

To Julie, my wonderful wife; to our children,
Ryan, Kaicie, and Jake; and to my parents,
Norman and Lou Ann.

—B.A.

CONTENTS

ACKNOWLEDGMENTS

The authors would like to extend special thanks to the people who laid the foundation of the Project Management for Profit system:

- Joe Cornwell, cofounder of Setpoint, for his visions of new ways to run a business

- Joe VanDenBerghe, cofounder of Setpoint, for his insights and innovations in developing and maintaining the internal business systems that Project Management for Profit requires

The Joes took a huge leap of faith when they decided to run Setpoint in such a radically different way from most businesses. Their methods and philosophies are the basis of the Project Management for Profit system, and for that we extend our sincere gratitude.

We would also like to send a special thank-you to every one of the dedicated and hardworking team members that we've worked with over the years at Setpoint. Without your faith in and dedication to the system, it simply wouldn't work.

Special thanks also go out to John Case for herding and shaping all of our thoughts and ideas into readable text. We couldn't have done it without you, John.

We'd like to thank our editor, Tim Sullivan, as well as the whole team at Harvard Business Review Press. Without their insights and efforts, this book would never exist. And we want to thank James Levine and the rest of the team at the Levine Greenberg Literary Agency for shepherding us through the process of bringing this book to life.

NO MORE HEADACHES, HYPERTENSION, AND HEARTBURN

Does your work involve projects? If it does, welcome to the future. Projects are everywhere these days.

One reason is the amazing proliferation of project-based companies in today's economy. Construction firms, software companies, architectural and engineering firms, marketing and public relations and consulting businesses, designers, machine builders, event managers, IT systems companies, you name it. Sometimes it seems as if the whole world is getting more project based, since people can now collaborate easily over large geographic distances.

All these project-based enterprises earn their living—or try to—by taking on discrete, custom jobs and bringing them to a successful, profitable end. In other words, they live or die with the quality of their project management, from the owner or CEO on out to the line manager running the most recent job.

And it isn't just project-based businesses that depend on good project management. Operating companies—manufacturers, retailers, insurers, media companies, health-care organizations, even nonprofits and government agencies—all are facing rapidly changing markets. They have to adapt quickly. And how do they adapt? You guessed it: projects. They create new products and services, develop or buy new equipment, institute new procedures and systems, launch new marketing campaigns, build new facilities. Little wonder that most large operating companies have a project management office and need a lot of talented project managers. Without successful projects, they'd wind up stuck in the mud—and left behind in the new world of competition.

All these developments mean that one job is going at a premium: that of the project manager. The need for well-trained and savvy project managers has never been greater than it is today. Online job searches for project management positions invariably list a multitude of openings, both domestic and overseas. Complex technologies, never-ending infrastructure enhancements, and the opening of global markets present seemingly endless opportunities for somebody with the right capabilities. Very likely, project management will continue to be one of the most sought-after skill sets in the business world, making it a highly lucrative pursuit for those who have what it takes.

But if you have been around project management for any length of time, you know the profession's sorry little secret. Good project managers—*really* good ones—are hard to find. Even harder to find are project management methods that actually work.

The reason is that project management is so tough. Every project comes with a defined scope, a budget, and a schedule.

At first it looks so—well, manageable. The team plunges in, with the boss or the project manager as a vigilant supervisor. But then comes trouble. The job begins spinning out of control. The scope creeps upward. Costs skyrocket. The schedule turns into a running joke. Managers see that things are going wrong, but they can't figure out what to do about it. They get headaches, hypertension, and heartburn, not to mention stomach ulcers and prematurely gray hair.

If you think we're overstating the case, take this little ten-question test. Versions of it appear in a lot of project management books, so we can't claim originality. Just see whether you recognize your own—or your company's—experience in the questions.

1. Have you ever been over budget on a project?

2. Have you ever exceeded the timeline on a project?

3. Do your projects rapidly go to 90 percent complete and then seem to hover there forever?

4. When your projects are finished, does it usually take more than thirty days to figure out whether you made or lost money? (And then does the accountant or the finance department adjust the numbers at least once more after that?)

5. Have you ever lost money on a sure-thing project without any idea why?

6. Do you notice that scope or feature creep is part of every project you work on—and that you don't know what to do about it? Have you ever lost a bundle on scope creep gone wild?

7. Does a carelessly planned project take three times as long as you thought? And a well-planned project twice as long?

8. Have you ever been too embarrassed to review projects for schedule and budget success or failure after completion?

9. Do the members of your teams have a cavalier attitude toward budgets and schedules because it isn't their job?

10. If you had to live solely off of the profitability of your projects, would you have starved to death a long time ago?

Honest answers to these questions typically produce a lot of mumbling, red-faced business owners and project managers. At one time in our lives we could have answered yes to nearly every one. If you answered yes to only two or three, trust us: you need this book.

Of course, we don't mean to oversimplify. Project management produces successes as well as failures. But even a success can easily be compromised. Listen to the saga of one project manager we know well, who was handling an amusement park construction job in Las Vegas.

> We were building four midsize amusement rides for installation on the Vegas strip. It was a short-trigger schedule, and things had been tense from the moment the contract was signed, fourteen months earlier. The customer planned to open a new casino in conjunction with the new rides. One thing you have to know about Las Vegas and casino construction: the casino is the customer's money machine. Anything that gets in the way of turning on the money machine is a serious

problem. At one point, one of the customer's representatives suggested bluntly that failure to complete the
project on time could land me in a shallow hole in the
Nevada desert. I don't think he meant it literally, but
I took it seriously anyway. Delay was definitely not an
option.

We worked seven days a week and around the clock
from Memorial Day to Labor Day to bring things in
on time. And now we were at the finish line. A local
TV newscaster came out to interview members of
our team. Our company's vice president came out
for the ribbon-cutting ceremony. At the ceremony,
the customer's gruff construction manager made his
way through the crowd—and to everyone's surprise
opened his arms and gave us bear hugs. "We did it!" he
said. "Great job! I'd work with you boys any day on any
project!" There were celebratory toasts, photo sessions,
long luncheons in the construction trailers, and smiles
on every face. We got the hero treatment again when
we returned to our home office.

About two months later, the vice president of
finance summoned us. We expected congratulations
and a final accounting of how much profit we had
made on the Vegas victory. But the look on his face
wasn't congratulatory. "I need you to explain to me in
detail," he said brusquely, "how you managed to lose
a million dollars on the Vegas project. I can't believe
that this project was such a disaster." We had figured
we would net half a million or so, in spite of all of the
challenges. But we didn't count the ancillary costs that
weren't rolled into the project until long after we had

finished the job. We didn't count the allocation of
overhead. We didn't realize there was a lag of several
weeks before labor was properly tallied and expensed
against the project.

In the end, we understood we had lost a ton of
money. Our hero status was rescinded, and we were now
the goats who had "nearly bankrupted the company."

Conventional project management systems and tools often
fail to tell you in a timely manner whether you are making
money, or what to do about it if you're not. It may seem as if
project managers have too much information, with all the
charts and schedules and other printouts they carry around,
but in fact they have too little. Sure, project managers might
get financial reports now and then, but those reports are rarely
helpful. The typical project is like the Vegas amusement park
rides: nobody really knows whether the whole thing is profitable or on budget until the finance folks get around to the final
accounting. And in most cases, that's usually long after the project is complete.

And then there are scheduling problems. One of us, Roger,
was once a brand-new project manager for a software company
and had just created a big, detailed schedule for a product
that was in the early stages of development. Here's what happened next:

I was in a meeting with the lead developer, going
through the details of the required tasks and their
place in the master schedule. After an awkward hour of
trying to discuss realistic deliverables and time frames,
the developer finally boiled over. "I don't know why
you're wasting my time with this crap!" he exclaimed.

"Everybody knows the schedule is a joke, and we pay no attention to it. This type of software development is impossible to predict or schedule. It will be done when it's done." And the meeting was over.

The reaction, unfortunately, isn't unusual. The people who develop schedules often get little or no input from the individuals who have to deliver the finished product. Sometimes the only schedule information that the project team ever hears is the final due date. Given human nature, people tend to disregard schedules that they haven't been consulted on and that they deem unreachable. They figure they'll do the best job they can, and it "will be done when it's done." That, by the way, is a terrifying phrase for any project manager to hear. Yet most have heard it more than once.

At the software company, Roger needed to parse out the required tasks so that they would be reasonably predictable and thus able to be scheduled, and at the same time get the development team to buy into the schedule. He needed to change the way everyone looked at the tasks necessary to complete the project, and he needed to devise some tangible and reachable goals for the team to shoot for. At the time, alas, he wasn't sure how to go about all that.

Financial and scheduling problems—and of course they're related—lead to a whole host of dismal consequences.

- Let's say you're behind schedule on your project. The natural impulse is to throw money at the problem—*firing the money cannon,* we call it. More hours. More bodies. Bring in outside subcontractors. But will all that undermine profitability? You fear it will, but you don't really know. (You do know that there is no line item on the budget labeled "fire the money cannon.") Because you don't know where you stand financially, you control what you can—the delivery date.

- Or maybe you're over budget. Quick: cut back on expenses. But which ones? And by how much? Where did the problem come from, anyway? And when did it actually happen? Again, chances are you don't know, because your project management system doesn't tell you.

- Or say your customer is requesting several change orders. Can you accurately estimate the cost of each one and then track their effect on profitability as your project goes along? Probably not. Is your team aware of where they stand financially at any given time, so that they can guard against this kind of scope creep? Again, probably not.

Too often, projects are managed by hope and by prayer. *We hope it will get done on time and on budget. We pray that nothing (else) will go wrong. But we don't really know, because we don't have a good system of tracking the financial effect of every move we make.* In fact, if your system doesn't let you connect money spent with labor used on a near-real-time basis, you're in a pickle, because you'll be unable to use either lever to complete the project.

Project-based companies pay a terrible price for these failures. Many go out of business. Setpoint, the company that created the whole Project Management for Profit system, is on its third generation of competitors, and it has been in operation just twenty years. If a project-based company isn't yet out of business, it may be among the walking dead—you know, making up the deficit of the last project with the advance money for the next one. This is not a viable long-term solution. It is living on cash flow rather than on profits.

Operating companies, too, pay a price for poor project management, though it may not be immediately visible. Has anyone in an operating company ever seen the installation of a new IT system or the construction of a new facility come in on schedule and on budget? What about a new-product launch or a full-scale Web site redesign? Delays and cost overruns are endemic nearly everywhere, regardless of context, and so the projects eat up what would otherwise be discretionary cash.

But things don't have to be this way. This book will show every company owner and project manager, no matter how small his or her business, how to run projects differently. Using the system we have developed, the owner or manager and their teams will be able to:

- Accurately track progress on a weekly basis—not just milestones and budget but profitability—and make whatever course corrections are necessary.

- Let everyone working on the project see exactly how they're doing, and harness their ideas about how to fix whatever goes wrong. (Something always does.)

- Identify the need for change orders as they happen, and incorporate each one into the overall project financials.

- Communicate weekly with customers—bad news as well as good—so that customers are never surprised or outraged by enormous changes at the last minute. (Ditto for senior management, which also doesn't like surprises.)

- Use a detailed database of past projects for calculating costs, hours, and so forth, so that budgets are as accurate as they can possibly be.

Business is a serious, competitive contest, and losers have to find something else to do. Nobody would play any other competitive sport professionally without a real-time scoreboard, because they wouldn't know whether they were winning or losing. Our fail-safe system of project management provides every project manager—and everyone else working on the project—with just such a scoreboard. Literally.

Please note that when we refer to the Project Management for Profit *system*, we're not talking about a software package or some unconventional set of accounting methods. The system is a set of methodologies and metrics that help you monitor and thus promote efficiency, teamwork, and profitability. All of the philosophies, methods, and formulas you will need to implement the system are included in this book. Once you have mastered the theories behind the system, it's simply a matter of building your calculation spreadsheets and plugging in your data to learn where your projects stand financially at any given time.

In the first three chapters, we'll tell you a little about where the Project Management for Profit system came from, and about the principles it is based on. That will help you understand exactly why and how it works. As you'll see, it was developed from the ground up by practical engineers and businesspeople looking for a solution to some pressing project management problems. No ivory tower here.

Then we'll get to the heart of the matter: several chapters showing exactly how the system operates and how you can use it both to monitor your jobs and to take corrective actions when things threaten to go off course. We'll also show you how to share critical information with your team, so that everyone (not just you) is watching out for scope creep, delays, and cost overruns. We'll discuss how to handle big projects, what to do if your project has no external customer, and how to ensure that the system always operates at peak performance levels. By the time you finish the book, we hope you will be prepared to implement Project Management for Profit in your own company— prepared, in other words, to keep your own projects on track and on budget.

Today, project management is more than a position or a career. It has become a mind-set, and it turns up in every corner of the business world. Every company is trying to manage its resources as closely as possible, and project management is an essential part of that effort. But not every business has experienced project managers on staff or access to the sophisticated software and tools that professional project managers use. Owners of small and midsize companies in particular must constantly monitor and manage their business efforts as projects, much as a project manager does. If this book can help them run their projects and their businesses more effectively, we will have achieved our goal.

One more thing: if you need information or guidance beyond what the book offers, please visit our Web site, www.pm4profit.com. We will be glad to help with any questions or concerns.

PART ONE

LAYING THE FOUNDATION

CHAPTER 1

HOW THE KONG RIDE LED TO PROJECT MANAGEMENT FOR PROFIT

In the beginning were Arrow, two engineers named Joe, and the Kong ride.

Arrow was Arrow Dynamics, formerly Arrow Development and then Arrow-Huss, a company with a storied history and a propensity for running out of money. Based near Salt Lake City, Arrow made roller coasters. Its specialty was big, fancy rides, for the likes of Disneyland, Six Flags, and Knott's Berry Farm. (Walt Disney himself had been a part owner of the company at one point.) Arrow was one of the most respected names in the industry, responsible for many roller-coaster innovations that are widely used today. People throughout the amusement park world knew that an innovative Arrow ride was always a big moneymaker.

The company, unfortunately, was not a big moneymaker. Its business model was to secure five or six contracts each year, build the rides, and see how much money was left at year-end. Sometimes there were profits; more often red ink. The business weathered two bankruptcies and changed hands three times during the 1980s. It was constantly scrambling to get the next contract so it could stay alive. Everyone was profiting from Arrow's rides, it seemed, except Arrow itself. (Arrow's final bankruptcy would come in 2001, when its assets were sold to a competitor.)

In the early 1990s, two talented young engineers came to work at Arrow.

Joe Cornwell was a mechanical engineer, born in 1959, a graduate of Christian Brothers University. At six feet seven and 280 pounds, Cornwell was a man who stood out in a crowd. He had a dark sense of humor, often coming out with phrases such as, "The best thing about people is that they are biodegradable." At the same time, he had an unusual ability to get along with nearly everyone he met. At work, he favored T-shirts and cargo shorts. In his off-hours he enjoyed riding dirt bikes.

Joe VanDenBerghe was an electrical engineer. VanDenBerghe was closer to average height and weight, and he wore a mustache. Born in 1961, he grew up in southern Utah and earned his engineering degree from Utah State University. VanDenBerghe held a pilot's license and later would own his own plane. He liked to tell funny stories, but his coworkers felt that he suffered from poor comic timing. It usually took them a minute to get the joke.

The pair met at Arrow and hit it off right away, working together on several projects. They discovered that they shared a taste for technical engineering challenges. They shared a distaste for Arrow's style of management.

At one point, Cornwell and VanDenBerghe found themselves assigned to the most complex ride Arrow had ever tackled. Cornwell was the project engineer. VanDenBerghe was the lead engineer for electrical and controls. The ride would be known as Kong. At its heart was a 30-foot-tall King Kong robotic figure that interacted with theme park patrons, including giving them a dose of his banana breath. The ride part of the project was a tram car that carried people past the giant ape. As it passed, Kong would grab the tram, shake it, and then drop it toward the ground. The tram's complex mechanisms rocked the vehicle during the shaking episode and then simulated a free fall when Kong dropped it. The mechanism stopped the tram gently as it approached the ground.

The company had assembled an all-star team to build the ride, and Cornwell and VanDenBerghe were happy to be a part of it. The technical challenges were immense—just what they liked. They watched the project clear one daunting technical hurdle after another.

But the celebrations after each accomplishment were notably short-lived. Managers began accosting the team with financial and scheduling demands. Team members began to fear that, in the grand Arrow tradition, the project was losing money. Every so often, they achieved a milestone that triggered a payment, and an accounting report would eventually show a profit or loss—usually a loss—for that portion of the project. By the time the report came out, however, the project was already two or three milestones further along. On some Arrow projects, the entire project was completed months before *any* accounting reports were received.

The accounting—and the lectures from management about tightening up and moving faster—smacked of Monday-morning quarterbacking. None seemed to help the project succeed.

And indeed, how could they? The discussions of progress and the accounting figures often revealed worthwhile information, but by then it was mostly irrelevant. If team members had known more of the information while doing that part of the job, it would have been more useful. Instead, the team got a postgame report from the accounting department.

Cornwell and VanDenBerghe began talking intently about the situation. Wouldn't it be nice, they asked one another, to know that your army was running low on ammunition during the battle, as opposed to learning afterward that it had run out of ammo in the middle? Wouldn't it be good to make course corrections during a sailing voyage, rather than waiting to reach land and then figuring out where you wound up?

Arrow's all-star team eventually completed the Kong ride. It was one of a kind, another technical marvel that would last for years. (Installed at Universal Studios in Florida, it has since been replaced by a Revenge of the Mummy ride.) True to form, the buyer made millions on the ride. Arrow lost millions in building it. Cornwell and VanDenBerghe figured there had to be a better way.

Searching for a New System

Their frustration growing, Cornwell and VanDenBerghe decided to undertake some engineering projects on their own. The automotive air bag industry was growing rapidly at the time, and one of the major companies in the business was located nearby. The two engineers worked their contacts to secure a few design-and-build contracts for automation modules to be used in air bag manufacture. Resigning from Arrow, they began to devote full time to building a new company, which they christened Setpoint.

Setpoint thrived from the beginning. Several of Cornwell and VanDenBerghe's colleagues from Arrow joined them. More contracts came the company's way. The small group moved from the garage that was Setpoint's birthplace into a rented building that provided both workshop and office space. Before long Cornwell and VanDenBerghe had regular revenue, schedules to meet, and budgets to balance.

Before long, too, they were taking on another former colleague from Arrow—one of this book's authors, Joe Knight. Knight wasn't an engineer. He held an MBA in finance from the University of California at Berkeley, and he had worked for Ford Motor Company and several other firms. But he seemed to have the right first name. Quickly, the trio became known to their colleagues as the Joes. In 2001, *Inc.* magazine ran a feature article on Setpoint by editor at large Bo Burlingham. "Other companies have senior managers," Burlingham wrote. "Setpoint has 'the Joes.'"

From the beginning, each Joe had his own role to play. Cornwell was the visionary, the dreamer, regularly coming up with bold ideas designed to establish the company firmly in the custom automation business. He was also the social linchpin of the group, constantly using his network of contacts to find more business. VanDenBerghe was the consummate engineer, establishing and continually refining Setpoint's internal systems, tools, and methodologies. VanDenBerghe didn't like gray areas. If he could make everything as black-and-white as possible, he believed, the company's decisions would be more scientific and thus more accurate. Knight, for his part, brought the financial knowledge and business experience that the others lacked.

Despite their success in launching the company, the Joes were worried. Like Arrow, Setpoint was a project-based business. And projects, they knew from their experience, were always iffy. Setpoint had to be run differently. Nobody wanted another Kong-type project.

Some changes were obvious. Arrow, constantly short of cash, was perennially late in paying its suppliers. Some of those suppliers quit doing business with the company. Others required cash up front before they would ship. One result of Arrow's shaky relationships with vendors was periodic interruptions in the supply of parts and services. That played havoc with project schedules. Another result: inflated costs. Vendors priced their wares high, hoping to get back some of what they had lost on earlier Arrow jobs. Customers, meanwhile, sensed Arrow's desperate need for cash and used it against the company in price negotiations.

Setpoint, the Joes determined, would always pay its bills on time. And it would cultivate close working relationships with customers.

Solving the basic problem of projects, however, was more challenging. For instance, the Joes asked themselves this:

> What would be required for us to know what a project
> was really going to cost? Wouldn't it be great if we
> could see real costs in detail as the project goes along?
> The purpose of a business, after all, is to make money,
> and if we don't know our costs, we won't have a clue
> regarding our profit.

And this:

> What about knowing as we went along how long the
> project was really going to take? And whether it would
> really meet the customer's specifications without a lot
> of change orders or budget overruns? Wouldn't that be
> great, too?

Project managers, they felt, lived in a world of unreality, held together by hope and prayer. What would it take to bring projects into the real world, to create a sense of commitment and discipline among everyone involved, to keep everyone focused on the right priorities?

Maybe, they decided, we could design a project management system that would do all that. We're engineers, aren't we? And that's what engineers do: design systems.

The design specs for this system would include all that real-time knowledge just mentioned. They would also include several other requirements for successful projects:

1. The system would be proactive rather than reactive. It would allow a project team to get on top of what needed to be done, rather than continually putting out fires.

2. The system would help project teams achieve both short-term and long-term goals, and it would tie financial scorekeeping directly to those goals. It would enable the company to reward people for hitting accurately determined project targets.

3. It would allow for regular, accurate communication with customers, in words they could understand.

4. It would build in commitment and discipline from top to bottom, overcoming the complacency that often shows up in the early stages of a long job.

5. Finally, it would help people focus on tasks that were important rather than urgent.

That last requirement may require a word of explanation, because project managers and team members are forever concentrating on whatever seems most urgent. That practice, the

Joes believed, was exactly wrong, and was at the heart of a lot of project management troubles.

Stephen R. Covey's famous time management system divides tasks into the two-by-two matrix shown in figure 1-1. In his book *The 7 Habits of Highly Effective People*, Covey argues that all critical work is completed in quadrant 2, the one labeled Important/ not urgent. The Joes believed that every project management activity, when properly executed, should fall into quadrant 2. Their reasoning was simplicity itself. Every project management activity is important, or else it shouldn't be done at all. And every task should be completed before it becomes urgent. If a task is suddenly urgent, it is likely to be expensive—and the project manager has failed.

FIGURE 1-1

The Covey time management matrix

Quadrant 1	Quadrant 2
Important/urgent	Important/not urgent
• Crises • Pressing problems • Deadline-driven projects	• Prevention activities • Relationship building • Recognizing new opportunities • Planning, recreation
Quadrant 3	**Quadrant 4**
Urgent/not important	Not urgent/not important
• Interruptions, some calls • Some mail, some reports • Some meetings • Proximate, pressing matters • Popular activities	• Trivia, busywork • Some mail • Some phone calls • Time wasters • Pleasant activities

Source: Stephen R. Covey, *The 7 Habits of Highly Effective People* (New York: Free Press, 2004), 151.

Now that they had their design specs formulated, it was time for the real work to begin. The ambitious specifications had to be rolled together into a workable business system that everyone could easily understand and use. Of course, it also had to integrate directly, in real time, with Setpoint's accounting system. Little did they know how big that factor would become.

To understand it, we'll have to take a brief detour into the world of accounting.

CHAPTER 2

WHY THE ACCOUNTING DEPARTMENT IS YOUR WORST ENEMY

In the United States, a mammoth code known as Generally Accepted Accounting Principles (GAAP, pronounced "gap") spells out the procedures governing accounting. GAAP comprises thousands of pages' worth of rules and guidelines. A private organization called the Financial Accounting Standards Board (FASB) monitors GAAP and regularly updates it. Most other countries have something similar.

Every publicly traded company in the United States must maintain its books according to the rules of GAAP. Privately held companies aren't required to do so, but if a private company wants to establish a credit line or get a loan from a bank, it will often have to show the bank's loan officer a set of financial statements compiled or audited according to GAAP. When Joe Cornwell and Joe VanDenBerghe started Setpoint, they hired a certified public accountant to set up the company's books. Like any self-respecting CPA, he followed GAAP's rules in doing so.

Cornwell, trained as a mechanical engineer, didn't know accounting. But he decided he would learn. He talked to the accountant. He bought some textbooks. Then he began meeting every Wednesday night with his friend Joe Knight, the finance expert, who at that point hadn't yet joined Setpoint. They got together at the small building that served as Setpoint's combined office and shop.

Cornwell also wanted to share some financial data with his employees. The group at the time included his partner, Joe VanDenBerghe; Cornwell's father, who worked part-time; and a few others. Arrow had shared virtually no financial information with the people running its projects, and Cornwell believed that the projects had suffered for it. He wasn't about to make the same mistake. But he wanted some advice from Knight on how to go about creating an open-book company.

At one of the meetings with Knight, Cornwell put an equation on the whiteboard. It looked like this:

$$\frac{\text{Sales} - \text{Stuff to buy}}{\text{Aggregate remainder}}$$

Then he proceeded to explain it. "Setpoint's business, its projects, are custom-built machines. So when we take on a contract to build a machine, we have sales.

"Then we have to buy the stuff we need to build the machine. Parts and materials. Subassemblies that we contract out. Technical services. Financially speaking, all I really want to focus on with my employees is how much is left over from the sales after we buy the stuff." Cornwell, who had not yet learned the language of accounting, had christened this number *aggregate remainder*. He went on to say that the higher the aggregate remainder, the better for everybody. There would be more money left over to pay the employees, and there was a better chance that he as an owner would make a profit.

Knight agreed with the logic. He observed that the usual term for aggregate remainder was *gross profit*. Cornwell got a gleam in his eye. "Hah. That's where I've got you," he said. "Gross profit is supposed to include labor costs, not just stuff to buy." Setpoint's accountant, following the rules of GAAP, had explained this to him. Cornwell had decided that accounting was crazy.

The definition of gross profit wasn't the only problem in his view. The accountant also followed GAAP rules in determining how far along a project was in financial terms—that is, how much revenue could be credited to it at a particular point along the way. GAAP's method was simple: determine the money you've spent as a percentage of the project's total budget. Then multiply the expected total revenue from the project by that percentage. Half the budget spent? Credit yourself with half the revenue and half the budgeted profit! Knight confirmed that the accountant was correct, according to GAAP. But Cornwell wasn't buying this, either. "Insane," he growled. "It makes no sense."

Intuitively, Joe Cornwell had put his finger on the two major reasons conventional accounting isn't well suited to project-based companies or to tracking projects in operating companies. In this chapter we'll take a detailed look at each one. It will help you see why you can't trust conventional financial reports—and why the Project Management for Profit system bypasses GAAP for the purposes of running projects.

Calculating Gross Profit

In a conventional GAAP-approved income statement, the top line is always labeled *Sales* or *Revenue.* If you run a small, cash-based retail store—a farm stand, say—your revenue for the month of August is simply the amount of money customers paid you for the fruits and veggies and eggs they bought in August.

Most companies, of course, are more complex. They usually invoice their customers for the products or services they deliver. The customers typically pay those invoices a month or two later—well after they received the products or services. Accountants long ago decided that they would record (or "recognize") revenue when a company *earned* it, not when the company got paid. If a manufacturer ships a truckload of gas grills worth $250,000 to a retailer's warehouse in April and sends the retailer an invoice on April 30, it has earned that $250,000 in April. It gets to include that figure on the revenue line of its April income statement regardless of when the customer might decide to pay the bill.

Often, of course, accountants have to exercise judgment about when to record revenue. Let's imagine that Acme Heating & Ventilating sells a rooftop air-conditioning unit to another business, and that the sale price includes a three-year service contract. Technically, Acme hasn't earned the full sale price until the three years are up, but it probably has earned most of the sale price as soon as it installs the unit. GAAP spells out guidelines for this kind of situation. Individual companies' accountants develop policies consistent with those guidelines and then apply the policies to their own business. Acme's policies might allow it to recognize 70 percent of the sale price when it sells the unit and 10 percent each year thereafter as the service contract is earned.

Project-based companies have their own challenges in determining when to recognize revenue, as Cornwell understood. We'll get to that in a moment.

First, let's continue on down the income statement. The second line, invariably, is *cost of goods sold* (COGS) or *cost of services* (COS). Revenue minus COGS or COS gives us the third line: *gross profit* (often called gross margin). Gross profit is a critical number in any business. In effect, it's the pot of money available to cover all the general expenses you incur in running the business plus whatever net profit is left over for the owners. Here's how all these items might look on a highly simplified income statement (which ignores taxes, among other things):

Revenue	$100,000
COGS (or COS)	– 80,000
Gross profit	20,000
Selling, general, and	
administrative expenses (SG&A)	– 10,000
Net profit	$10,000

Given the importance of gross profit, it matters a lot not only when you recognize revenue but also what items you include in COGS or COS. GAAP is pretty clear on that score, too. COGS or COS is supposed to include the *direct* costs of manufacturing the goods or delivering the services, including labor costs. A pizza shop, for instance, would include the cost of ingredients and other supplies, plus the cost of paying the kitchen help, the counterpeople, and so on.

Other expenses—rent, utilities, advertising, and the like—are *indirect* costs. They apply to the whole business rather than to making and delivering the pizza itself. They are included farther down the income statement, under selling, general, and administrative expenses (SG&A), which are sometimes labeled operating expenses (OE).

Cornwell didn't like it.

In fact, he found it almost offensive. COGS, he figured, should be a *variable* cost, one that depended on the size and specifications of Setpoint's projects and thus varied with revenue. SG&A should be *fixed* costs, everything that didn't vary with the amount of revenue.* In Cornwell's mind, labor was a fixed cost. It wasn't just an item on an income statement, after all; it was real people. He wasn't going to hire and fire his employees depending on the vagaries of revenue in a given month. He wasn't going to call them in or send them home depending on how much work there was that day. People had to eat. You had to pay them a regular wage or salary. The worst thing a business could do, he believed, was to lay people off.

Sure, maybe he would add a temporary contractor or two if he needed help on a big project, and that could be part of COGS. But real labor, Setpoint staff labor, should be treated as part of SG&A. That was the company's core team, and it wouldn't vary with the amount of revenue coming in. If you treated it as part of COGS, you wouldn't get an accurate picture of your real costs.

(By the way, if you're thinking that this is why you've always disliked accounting and finance, here's a shameless plug: pick up a copy of Karen Berman and Joe Knight's book, *Financial Intelligence.* It will help you understand the language of business in a way that doesn't require any understanding of debits, credits, or GAAP.)

---

*This is how engineers think. It isn't how accountants think. According to GAAP, both COGS and SG&A can easily include fixed *and* variable costs. For instance, COGS includes the cost of parts, which is variable because it depends on how much you're producing in any given month. But in a big company, COGS would also include lease payments on a manufacturing facility, which is a fixed cost. SG&A, meanwhile, would include lease payments on the company's headquarters, a fixed cost. Yet SG&A also includes sales commissions, which are definitely a variable cost.

Recognizing Project Revenue

The second problem Cornwell had was how to recognize revenue when a project was under way. His accountant said he had to recognize it by calculating the percentage of costs spent compared to total costs. That's what GAAP required. This seemed dangerous to Cornwell, and he was right.

Here's why. Let's assume that Setpoint has just won a major project through a competitive bid. The company prepared its bid by estimating the project's costs in detail and then adding in a reasonable profit. For the sake of this example, we'll say that Setpoint priced the project at $5 million. In reality, the number would never be so round; the price would probably be something like $5,099,237. (Clark, Setpoint's sales rep, always puts the lucky number 7 in his bids.) That would help persuade the customer that Setpoint had really done its homework in determining costs. But $5 million makes our math easier.

So the price is $5 million and the estimated total cost is $4 million. A simple preliminary project statement looks like this:

Project revenue	$5,000,000
Total costs	– 4,000,000
Project profit	$1,000,000

As you can see, the company is planning a 20 percent margin on this one: $1 million profit divided by $5 million in revenue.

Winning bid in hand, Setpoint starts work on the project, which is supposed to last eighteen months. Three months later, it has completed the initial layout and design for the job, and it has ordered all the necessary material. It has spent $2.25 million on Cornwell's "stuff to buy" plus $250,000 in labor costs, for a total expenditure of $2.5 million.

Now GAAP tells us how to record revenue and how to figure gross profit:

$$\text{Earned project revenue} = \frac{\text{actual cost to date}}{\text{total estimated costs}} \times \text{total project revenue}$$

Applying the equation to our example, we get earned revenue as follows:

$$\text{Earned project revenue} = \frac{\$2.5 \text{ million}}{4.0 \text{ million}} = 62.5\%$$

$$62.5\% \times \$5 \text{ million} = \$3.125 \text{ million}$$

So the profit associated with this project after three months would look like this:

	Months 1 through 3
Project revenue	$3,125,000
Project costs	– 2,500,000
Project profit	$ 625,000

Using the GAAP revenue recognition method based on cost, Setpoint's books would show $625,000 in profit on this project after three months. Compare that to the budgeted profit of $1 million. In just three months the company "earned" more than 60 percent of its budgeted profit! Time to celebrate, right? And maybe it's time to spend some of those profits.

The illusion of big profits is the reason so many project-based companies are among the walking dead. Company leaders see those profits early on and then go out and spend the money they think they have made. The Joes saw an example of this phenomenon firsthand. Early in Setpoint's history, the company outgrew its rented building, so it decided to build a steel-frame building that could accommodate its growth. Cornwell and others interviewed several local contractors and picked the one that seemed to understand how to run projects the Setpoint way.

They were mistaken. Setpoint paid the contractor a hefty down payment, and soon much of the building materials were being delivered to the site. Cornwell and Knight sat down with the project manager. "It's great to see the material already on site," said Cornwell. "It looks like you guys are really moving. Do you have an updated schedule?" He added that he hated contractors who get a big down payment, go out and buy everyone new pickups, and don't even have an updated schedule. Knight was desperately gesturing to Cornwell to shut up because the project manager had driven up in a brand-new pickup. But it was too late. They had the pickup but no updated schedule. The building was built, but that construction company was no longer in business by the time the project was complete.

Now back to the example of the $5 million project.

Using GAAP accounting, Setpoint would have recognized most of the profit on the project based on its best estimates at that time. The problem here is that three months really isn't very long on an eighteen-month project. The remaining costs, $1.5 million, are almost all labor for assembly and installation, plus a little for some final materials. This is the phase of the project when many things can change. Labor costs can exceed the budget. Design issues may require Setpoint to buy more material.

So let's assume that at the end of six months Setpoint has spent $3.5 million, including $2.5 million in materials costs and $1 million in labor. Much of the work is done, and Setpoint has a better idea of its total cost. It is now estimating that the total cost will come to $4.5 million. With revenue of $5 million and a cost of $4.5 million, Setpoint will earn a 10 percent profit margin on the project—not what it had hoped, but not too bad.

And what is the project's GAAP-based earned revenue at the end of six months? To calculate it, we'll use the same formula as before:

$$\text{Earned project revenue} = \frac{\$3.5 \text{ million}}{4.5 \text{ million}} = 77.8\%$$

77.8% × $5 million = $3.888889 million

So the profit associated with this project after six months would look like this:

	Months 1 through 6
Project revenue	$3,888,889
Project costs	– 3,500,000
Project profit	$ 388,889

Remember, at the end of month 3 we were seeing $625,000 in profit? Now it's a lot less. So let's look at the change in revenue and costs during months 4, 5, and 6:

	Months 4 through 6
Project revenue	$ 763,889
Project costs	– 1,000,000
Project profit	$ (236,111)

(Note that in accounting, parentheses or brackets indicate negative numbers.)

We made $625,000 in the first three months and lost $236,111 in the next three. The numbers suggest that we don't have the first idea what is going on with this project.

In our experience many companies panic at this six-month point. They might have spent some of that $625,000 in profit that their accountant told them they had earned. They also might have started other projects that are eating up some of their perceived profit. Now that they realize they "really" made less than $400,000 on the project, they suddenly decide it is time to rethink strategy.

Finding the Solutions

Joe Cornwell and Joe VanDenBerghe were engineers. They knew how to crunch numbers. When they saw the ramifications of this type of accounting, they knew that they didn't want to run their business like that. Moreover, they wanted to open the books to employees. How could they do that if they couldn't accurately measure profit on partially completed projects using the standard GAAP method? Nobody would believe a profit figure that seemed to bounce around inexplicably.

But there was a solution at hand. Joe Knight helped the two engineers understand that as a small privately held company, Setpoint did not need to follow GAAP. It could set up its books any way it wanted to. Later, it could format the data according to GAAP to satisfy bankers or anybody else who needed the books in that format.

Solution 1: Define COGS Differently

To solve the first problem, Setpoint decided that the cost of goods sold on its project books would include *only* materials, shipping, and contract labor hired specifically for a given project. All other labor, direct or otherwise, would be captured in operating expenses. That way, COGS would be closer to Cornwell's ideal of variable costs—stuff to buy.

Solution 2: Recognize Revenue and Profit Only on Labor

To solve the second problem, Setpoint decided to recognize revenue and profit on a project *only* on labor time, not on total costs. The Joes figured that the only way to earn real profit is to do the work. Ordering more than $2 million worth of materials at the start of a project takes a tiny fraction of the labor required to complete the project, so by this thinking, Setpoint would recognize only a tiny fraction of the profit at this point.

In the following chapter, we will describe the principles that the Joes developed to control a project. Starting with that chapter, we will try to refrain from any more discussion of GAAP-based accounting. But remember these two solutions, because they are central to the entire Project Management for Profit system.

CHAPTER 2 TAKEAWAYS

- GAAP accounting is rarely helpful in determining a project's profitability.

- The Project Management for Profit system makes two key adjustments to GAAP: it defines COGS only as outside purchases, and it recognizes revenue and profit only on the basis of labor hours. You may want to come up with a different set of adjustments to fit your own situation. You need not be constrained by GAAP.

CHAPTER 3

THE THREE PRINCIPLES OF CONTROL

Projects can quickly turn into nightmares. Here is a story told to us by an acquaintance we'll call Mike, who runs an excavating company.

> The project was a massive excavation for a public utility that was upgrading a major facility to accommodate new housing. The site plan showed a complex web of trenches where all of the new conduits and piping would be buried. In our winning bid, we planned for a crew of eighteen laborers and six earthmovers with operators. The contract had a nice on-time bonus clause that would boost our profit significantly, so we were highly motivated to stay on task.
>
> The engineers had carefully staged the project plan. We would need to dig individual trenches at specific points of the schedule, wait for other contractors to install

the underground utilities, and then quickly refill the trenches. In theory, this staged-completion plan would make the site more manageable for all the contractors, since we all had to complete our tasks in conjunction with each other and in a relatively small area.

As the first phase of the project was in full swing, we soon realized that the gyrations required to maneuver through the job site's tight quarters were eating us alive and destroying our schedule. Often we would need to get other contractors to move their equipment so we could move ours in to do our work. We were only two weeks into the eight-week project, and already we were nearly a week behind schedule.

I asked my foreman on the site what he thought might help us get back on track. He suggested we put a small crew on during the second shift and have them do much of the setup work for the day shift. Since the site would be empty, the night team could maneuver around much more easily. This sounded great, but my entire team was already committed, and no extra help was readily available. Again my foreman had a good suggestion. "I know that Sierra Excavating is kind of slow right now," he said, "and they have some good people. I bet they'd help us."

Sierra Excavating was a friendly competitor that had bid against us many times. We both won a reasonable share of the work, so there was no intensity to the rivalry. When I pitched the idea to Sierra's owner, he agreed to provide us with a flexible team that would work the second shift as required. My expectation was that this small team would need to work only four or five hours a night. I knew it was going to affect our profitability, but I figured if it helped us finish on time and cost no more than the amount of our on-time bonus, the project would still be financially successful. My stress level ticked down a few notches.

After the first week of the night shift, I asked the Sierra foreman for a tally of his team's hours for the week. The total was close to what I had expected, and we were back on schedule. I asked Sierra's office to send me an invoice, and they said that they would bill me monthly.

Over the next four weeks, Sierra regularly sent in their people as required. They did a great job on whatever my foreman asked them to do. Often the daily report from the site would include comments about the value of the night team. Unfortunately, I neglected to ask for the number of hours that Sierra was putting in each day. I just assumed it would be similar to the first week.

As we approached the project's last phase, I was confident that we would get it done on time and still make a reasonable profit, even though our on-time bonus would mostly go toward paying Sierra. Then, as I was going through my mail one day, I noticed an invoice from Sierra for the preceding month. I opened the invoice, looked down at the "amount due" total, and nearly had a heart attack. The total was more than triple what I had expected it to be. The hourly rates were what we had agreed upon, but the number of hours billed was way too high.

I called Sierra's billing department and explained my confusion. The office manager was nice, but she was adamant that the billed hours were accurate. She added that she had all the necessary backup documentation. I asked her to please send it over. Then I called my foreman. "Well," he said, "after I saw what they could do, I guess I did have them do quite a bit more work than we might have planned originally. But I had to do that in order stay on schedule so we can collect our bonus."

At that very second, I realized what I had done. I had given my foreman a blank check to use at his discretion. I had stressed the importance of collecting the bonus, and he had done everything in his power to meet the scheduled milestones. And we did meet them. But the cost was staggering.

We continued using Sierra for the last weeks of the project to ensure that we didn't lose our bonus, but we used them with much more discretion. In the end, not only did they get the whole bonus amount, they also got all our projected profit and then some. My company went into the red for about $10,000 on the project, all because I didn't keep tighter control.

As Mike recognized—a bit too late, unfortunately—the key to successful project management is staying in control.

To many project managers, of course, "control" seems like a fantasy. An illusion. They know that things will be delayed, that pieces of the job will turn out to be more difficult than anticipated, that unforeseen events will screw up schedules and budgets. Like our friend Mike, many of them resort to hoping for the best and praying that they have solved a problem, when all they have done is make it worse.

Other project managers, confronted with unknowns and unknowables, become yellers. They seem to think that if they yell at their teams long enough and hard enough, the project will get back on track. Threats and intimidation become their primary tools of control.

Neither of these is a particularly productive approach. Like Cornwell and VanDenBerghe, we think it's better to manage projects in good engineering fashion, minimizing the unknowns, making decisions as objectively as possible, focusing on facts rather than on feelings, and handling the important issues before they become urgent. This perspective suggests three fundamental principles for staying in control of projects.

Principle 1: The Buck Stops with the Project Manager

Many companies divide up operations and accounting. Project managers are responsible for running the projects; finance is responsible for tallying up the profits and the losses. That is how Arrow worked (or didn't work). In the excavation example, the foreman had responsibility for operations, the owner had responsibility for profitability, and neither man had all the information he needed to meet those responsibilities effectively. It's far better for project managers to have complete ownership of every aspect of a project from start to finish, including tracking financial progress. Project managers are responsible for planning, initiating, executing, and profiting from their projects. They should know exactly where a project stands financially at any given time throughout the course of the venture.

Here is a list of everything a Setpoint project manager is responsible for:

- The overall project plan—the big picture of how to get from A to Z.

- Budget development, monitoring, updating, and reporting weekly.

- Schedule development, monitoring, updating, and reporting weekly.

- Materials ordering and delivery logistics.

- Fulfillment of labor requirements.

- Task completion monitoring and reporting.

- Customer communications and relationship management.

- Intracompany communications (management team, interdepartment, etc.).

- Defending the project against scope creep and constantly clarifying the original scope of the project.

- Guardianship of the project's deliverables. This includes anything that is to be handed to the customer as part of the contract. Deliverables can range from an early concept sketch all the way to the final product.

- Ownership of a host of tasks that aren't easily defined, such as keeping everyone motivated, meshing the diverse skill sets and personalities of team members to achieve the best possible outcome, and constantly watching for the slightest hints of wildfires or surprises that can spin out of control.

- The final profitability of the project. This one naturally depends upon the smooth execution of all the other responsibilities. In most situations it's a key factor in determining the project's success.

Your company's list may vary somewhat, but if you are to be effective as a project manager, it should reflect the basic principle of no divided responsibilities. At no point should any project manager be able to say, "That wasn't part of my job."

Taken as a whole, these responsibilities form a complex integrated structure. Each is interdependent with others, and each must be constantly monitored. The project manager is responsible for making course corrections whenever anything threatens to throw the project off track. Like a helmsman steering a ship through the North Atlantic, project managers can't control where the icebergs will be. They need early-warning systems that tell them when they are in danger of running into one.

Principle 2: Project Managers Need Accurate, Timely Information

How on earth can an ordinary human being take on all these responsibilities and accomplish all these tasks? Well, one way is to share some of them with other members of the project team, a principle we will get to shortly. And in larger organizations, project managers are likely to have plenty of assistants to whom they can delegate many specific tasks. But one essential key to successful performance is good information, available at all times.

Most businesses need much the same data to track the financial status of their efforts. The two key items are generally materials and labor costs. Virtually every company has a method of capturing that information, ranging from handwritten logbooks to million-dollar business-management software packages. The method isn't important, so long as it suits your business and your budget. What's important is that the data is accurate and that you can get it in a timely manner. If you are working with data that's old, incomplete, or just plain wrong, then whatever system you use won't be adequate.

The Joes knew that, and like good engineers, they immediately drew up a list of design specs for the data-collection system that would be so critical to the project management methodology they envisioned:

1. It would need a full-featured, flexible *purchasing* system, including a materials tracking and pricing database, project designation, cost tracking, and purchase order generation.

2. It would need a simple yet comprehensive *time-tracking* system for the team's time clock—simple enough to be user friendly and comprehensive enough to track and accrue time to the projects or subsections of projects that each team member works on. The package would have to be able to sort and filter this data as required. (No software, of course, can track the time of people who don't enter their hours into the computer. The Joes made it mandatory for all Setpoint employees to enter their time every day as a condition for getting paid.)

3. It would need a *reporting* system allowing real-time access to the purchasing and time-tracking data. It would have to be able to produce reports telling a project manager exactly where he or she stood on materials expenditures and labor for any given project at any given time.

4. Setpoint already had a commercial accounting software package that was working well, and that package probably could not be integrated directly with the project management software. So there would need to be some level of *manual interface* between the two systems. The simpler the required interface, the better.

In addition to a rock-solid data-collection system, the Joes knew they would need a good scheduling tool to create and track Gantt charts and task lists. There were dozens of such packages readily available back then that could do the job. (There are even more today.)

Although there were many commercial software packages that might have fit this ambitious bill, the Joes determined that none had the complete feature set they felt was essential. As the resident software expert, Joe VanDenBerghe took on the task of developing a custom data-collection system. Together with contract programmers, he incorporated all the features that he and the others believed were necessary. Remarkably, Setpoint still uses an enhanced version of the same software today, though there are now even more comprehensive commercial packages available.

Every situation has different requirements, so we can't know exactly what methods or software tools may be best for your circumstances. Whatever your system, the following are the bare-minimum conditions it should meet:

1. It must be able to accurately accrue and report labor hours applied to specific projects.

2. It must be able to accurately accrue and report materials costs for specific projects.

3. All this data must be available in as close to real time as possible.

4. The data must be accurate and trustworthy. If it's not, none of your project metrics will be useful.

If your data system can deliver on those four requirements, you will have all of the information you need to implement the Project Management for Profit system.

Principle 3: Many Eyes Are Better Than Two, and Many Brains Better Than One

We're going to hold off on a detailed discussion of this principle for right now, because we'll get heavily into it in chapter 9. But the basics aren't hard to understand. If everyone on a project team sees (and learns to understand) the fundamental data showing how they are doing, they can spot trouble early. They can come up with ideas for solving problems, for saving money, and for getting things done slicker, quicker, and cheaper. They will understand why the project manager is pursuing path A rather than path B, and they'll help things along. Though ultimate responsibility rests with the project manager, he or she no longer is trying to sail the ship alone. There are many eyes on the lookout for icebergs, and many ideas about how to avoid them.

Mike, the excavator, charged his foreman with meeting the schedule. The foreman performed this task to perfection. He had no way of knowing that his actions were causing his company to lose money. And Mike had no way of knowing what was actually happening on the job site. Project Management for Profit wouldn't allow either situation to exist.

So those are the three principles of controlling a project. Now it's time to plunge in and see exactly how the system works.

CHAPTER 3 TAKEAWAYS

- No divided responsibilities! Project managers should be responsible for all phases of a project. No one should be able to say, "That wasn't part of my job." Every project has many twists and turns, so control is essential.

- Your organization must be able to produce accurate, timely information that people trust. If it can't, you are in trouble before the project even begins.

PART TWO

PUTTING THE SYSTEM TO WORK

WARNING:

OK, the easy part is over. It's time to get serious. You will need to pay close attention to the following five chapters—read and reread them, take notes, and spend time with the figures. Make sure that you clearly understand the methodologies that we're trying to convey before you dive into the nuts and bolts of the system. Then break out your calculator. Run through some of your own calculations using the formulas. Focus not just on the *what* of the system but on the *why*.

Is all this work worth the effort? We guarantee it. As you come to understand how to use the tools we describe, you will definitely become the project manager your mother always knew you could be.

CHAPTER 4

TRACKING YOUR MATERIALS

Now that you understand some of the background and principles governing the Project Management for Profit system, we're going to dive into the nitty-gritty of the system itself, the inner workings. We'll show you exactly how it operates, mostly through the use of simple examples. We'll describe how to derive the numbers you'll need, and how to use those numbers to keep your projects on track and on budget. If your projects are relatively small, you can track them manually using this system. If they're larger, you can check out our software on the Web or do your own programming. What matters is the way the system works, not the particular platform it works on.

We'll begin with what seems like the simplest part: estimating and tracking the cost of materials. Of course, nothing's ever simple when you're running a project, so we'll also point out some of the pitfalls you can run into along the way.

Note that the word *materials* in this chapter covers a lot of different stuff. It covers actual materials, like the lumber for building a house or the sheet metal for the casing on a machine.

It covers units or subassemblies that are contracted out. It also includes any outsourced services. If your project is a marketing campaign, your "materials" might include the cost of a free-lance copywriter or the services of a design shop. If it's a new piece of software, "materials" could include chunks of the programming purchased from outside contractors.

Because the category is so broad, many companies (including Setpoint) label it Cost of Goods Sold, or COGS, rather than calling it Materials. Just remember that the Project Management for Profit system, unlike GAAP, includes *no in-house labor costs* in COGS. It's *all* materials and services that you're buying from outside.

Why You Need Careful Tracking of Materials

If you're new to project management, you might think that tracking materials expenses or COGS wouldn't be particularly difficult or even particularly critical to a project's success. After all, you prepared a budget or bid before the project even began. If you did your homework at that point, you got firm prices or solid estimates on everything you would need to buy from somebody else. So you might not expect much variation on the COGS line.

As experienced project managers know, however, materials or COGS expenses are notorious as a source of budget overruns. Here are just a few of the ways it happens:

- **Prices change.** You made up your bid in the fall. In the spring, when you're actually ordering the materials, strange things happen. There's a sudden short-age of timber, asphalt, or steel. The design of the printed circuit boards that you need has changed. Some off-the-shelf components you intended to use have been discontinued. Whatever the cause, prices have gone up, and your supplier shrugs when you complain. "If I could sell it to you at last fall's price, I would. What do you expect me to do?"

We once had a project where materials prices rose 35 percent because of the ripple effect of a tsunami in Southeast Asia (no kidding). A few years later, the price of motor fuel rose past $4 a gallon, and our suppliers began adding a fuel surcharge to their bill— which, of course, we hadn't anticipated. The world is unpredictable.

- **You estimated the materials incorrectly.** You forgot that the architect specified Italian tile floors for the kitchen and basement as well as for the bathrooms. You didn't notice that the printer gave you a quote for ten thousand marketing brochures rather than the one hundred thousand you were planning on. Your engineers tell you that your plan to use regular steel for a large structure won't work; you need an expensive alloy instead. Such things seem to happen on every project.

- **Subcontractors cost more than you thought they would.** Sometimes that's a result of poor supervision, as in the case of Mike the excavator, reported in the previous chapter. More often, it's because the subcontractor's job turns out to be more difficult and time-consuming than anyone expected. The plumbing of the house turns out to be unusually challenging. The marketing copywriter has produced six drafts, but the client doesn't like any of them. The subcontractor and the client may eat part of the cost overruns on a project, but you're likely to have to eat some as well.

An accurate COGS estimate from week to week is essential to the Project Management for Profit system. The reason is simple: the system's key number is gross profit, and any project's gross profit is directly affected by COGS. If you get your COGS estimates wrong, then everything you calculate using those estimates will be wrong as well.

So let's look at how to go about tracking materials or COGS.

The COGS Report

Begin by imagining a good-sized project, one with $500,000 in materials costs. Since we're machine builders, we'll use COGS subcategories that we're familiar with—electrical work, fabricated parts, and mechanical contracting, along with that time-honored category always labeled miscellaneous. (At Setpoint, we typically budget miscellaneous as 10 percent of other materials costs.) For simplicity's sake, we'll examine only these few categories, and we'll keep the numbers round.

You, of course, should use categories that make sense for your business. Your categories may be both different and more numerous, the numbers won't be round at all, and you'll have to learn from experience how big your miscellaneous category is likely to be. But whatever the differences, the procedures will be exactly the same.

So let's say that the project is about 75 percent complete, and the project manager gets his weekly COGS report. If he's using the Project Management for Profit system, it will look something like figure 4-1.

Here's what each column represents:

Column A on the report is the simplest: it shows budgeted funds for COGS expenses in each subcategory. These figures come directly from the project bid or the initial

FIGURE 4-1

COGS Review Report							
Project - 5028			Customer - Sample			Report date - June 3	
Category	Bid $	Actual $	$ Remain in bid	Est $ to comp	Project % comp	% of bid	Total
Electrical	$125,000	$110,000	$15,000	$15,000	88.00%	88.00%	$125,000
Fabricated	$125,000	$150,000	($25,000)	$0	100.00%	120.00%	$150,000
Mechanical	$125,000	$100,000	$25,000	$15,000	86.96%	80.00%	$115,000
Misc	$125,000	$100,000	$25,000	$45,000	68.97%	80.00%	$145,000
Totals	$500,000	$460,000	$40,000	$75,000	85.98%	107.00%	$535,000
	A	B	C	D	E	F	G

budget. They are the benchmarks established at the outset. And they should never change. If you alter your budgeted figures during the course of a project, after all, you'll never be able to determine how good you are at budgeting. And we guarantee you will never get better.

Column B shows actual incurred expenses for each COGS subcategory. This data comes from the purchasing system's database in real time, so it is up to date as of the moment the report is run. This column includes project expenses that have already been paid, expenses invoiced by a supplier, and future expenses committed to through a purchase order. Your tracking system needs to pick up all of these costs in real time.

Column C represents the amount of COGS budget remaining. It is a calculated number: the system simply subtracts actual expenses from budgeted expenses and gives you the difference.

Column F, also a calculated number, shows actual COGS expenses as a percentage of budgeted COGS expenses.

Column D is the *estimated-to-complete* entry. This is the key column in the entire report, and it is where project managers earn their money. They must *estimate the remaining expenses* in each category.

If a project manager is really doing the necessary legwork here, it's highly unlikely that these estimates of remaining expense will be identical to the *remain-in-bid* total shown in column C. In fact, too much similarity between column C and column D usually indicates sloppy project management. You expect a project to have some variability in these expenses as the project progresses.

The reason is all those factors we mentioned earlier. Once a team is well into a project, things have started to happen. Unforeseen events have occurred. The estimated-to-complete entries shown in the COGS report should be real, up-to-date estimates based on the project's realities. If the number is the same as the number in column C, the project manager probably hasn't bothered to do this kind of updated estimate; he has just plugged in the remain-in-bid figure, so he probably doesn't know where things really stand.

The remaining columns, E and G, are both based on the figure in column D, which is why column D is so important:

- First, skip over to **column G**, the estimated total COGS. This is simply the sum of the actual incurred expenses (column B) and the project manager's estimated-to-complete total (column D). It's what he believes—as of right now—the real COGS figure will be when the project is complete.

- Now go back to **column E**, which shows the *percent-complete* calculation for COGS expenditures. This is the actual incurred expenses (column B) divided by the estimated total (column G). For example, look at the line item for mechanical expense. You'll see that we have already spent $100,000, and we have estimated that it will take $15,000 more to complete. The equation for that example looks like this:

$100,000	Incurred mechanical COGS expenses to date
15,000	Estimated COGS required to complete mechanical
$115,000	Total estimated mechanical COGS

$$\frac{\$100,000}{115,000} = 86.96\%$$

That's the percent-complete number we see in column E for mechanical.

It all can seem a little overwhelming at first. Once you begin using this kind of report regularly, though, your eye will glance over the numbers you already know and home in on the issues and concerns that the report reveals.

Analyzing the Data

In this report, for example, an experienced project manager might first compare the bottom line in column A to the bottom line in column G—the difference, in other words, between the original budgeted COGS total and the estimated COGS total as of right now. He would see that he is now projecting a COGS overrun of $35,000 to finish the job. The project has spent only $460,000 on materials up to this point (column B total), but he now expects to spend another $75,000 on materials to get to the finish line (column D total). That comes to $535,000, compared to the original budget of $500,000.

So where exactly is the overrun?

Electrical

Scanning the page, he looks first at the electrical subcategory. No trouble there: the budgeted figure in column A is the same as the estimated total in column G. So long as he has been assiduous in his real-time estimating, this subcategory is right on budget. The manager has $15,000 left in the budget to spend (column C) and estimates that he will need exactly that amount to complete the project (column D).

Fabricated

The fabricated materials subcategory, however, isn't on budget at all. In fact, column C shows a number in parentheses, signaling a cost overrun. He has already spent $25,000 more on this subcategory than was in the original budget or bid. The good news is that the project manager has entered $0 for his estimate to complete this line item (column D), so presumably he expects no more cash drain in the category. We have now identified a large portion of the $35,000 overrun.

Mechanical

A look across this line shows that we still have $25,000 left in the budget (column C), but the estimated-to-complete for that line item is only $15,000. If the project manager's estimate is correct, he'll realize a *gain* of $10,000 compared to budget on this subcategory. One note of caution here, however: be absolutely sure that your estimates are solid before you show this kind of gain in COGS expenses compared to budget. It's a common rookie mistake to recognize projected savings early, only to have surprises at the end of the job pop up and take it all back. Little is worse than having a projected gain turn into a loss because you were overoptimistic or shortsighted with your estimates.

Miscellaneous

The fourth and final subcategory is for miscellaneous materials. For machine builders like Setpoint, the miscellaneous line item might include items such as third-party inspections, fees for writing technical manuals, or rental of specialized equipment. In a construction project, it might include surveyors' fees or equipment moving costs. The figures on this line show that the project manager has spent $100,000 (column B) of the budgeted $125,000 (column A), so the report has calculated that he has $25,000 left in the budget (column C). However, the manager has entered $45,000 in the estimated-to-complete field (column D). In short, he expects to spend a total of $145,000 on miscellaneous materials, which amounts to a $20,000 overrun on the budget for that line.

In summary, the COGS analysis shows the source of the overrun:

Total estimated costs as of this week	(Over budget)/ under budget
Electrical	$ -0-
Fabricated	(25,000)
Mechanical	10,000
Miscellaneous	(20,000)
Total	$(35,000)

The project manager knows that as of now, his projected total COGS expenditure will be $535,000, for an overrun of $35,000. As we noted earlier, it's essential that this number be as accurate and up to date as possible. It's a key factor in formulating a true picture of the project's financial status. Constant surveillance on COGS can turn up a lot of red flags early. If you're lucky, you may even have enough warning to do something constructive about the situation.

CHAPTER 4 TAKEAWAYS

- The Project Management for Profit system tracks COGS (cost of goods sold) differently from GAAP. Do you remember what the difference is? If not, see chapter 2 for a refresher.

- The COGS worksheet you use must track the following items weekly:
  - COGS spent to date
  - COGS estimated-to-complete
  - Total estimated COGS compared to the original budget

- Once you understand the variance between the two, you can take action.

CHAPTER 5

MEASURING PERCENT COMPLETE

How far along is your project? Estimating progress is a key part of keeping the job on track and on budget.

Generally Accepted Accounting Principles, or GAAP, call for measuring the progress of a project by costs incurred—that is, by costs already spent or committed as a percentage of total forecast costs. We saw in chapter 2 why that method is a non-starter. Using GAAP, total costs include materials or COGS, and in many projects, you order most of your materials near the beginning of a project. You can be out half your total budget yet just barely getting started on the actual work.

Another method might be to compare actual labor expenses to total budgeted labor costs. That could work in theory, but it can be complex to put into practice. You have to know the different hourly rates for each kind of labor involved in the project, and you might have to compensate accordingly in your figuring. Architects and engineers, for example, are more expensive than construction laborers. If you do all your designing and engineering up front, you could easily get a skewed idea of how far along you are. In organizations with many labor cost categories, this method may be required. But in the Project Management for Profit system, we try to keep things as simple as possible.

Instead of measuring labor *costs*, we recommend using labor *hours* as your indicator. Add up the number of hours spent on your project so far. Divide by the total number of hours the project will require. The resulting percentage shows you how far along you are. You have used up one-quarter of the hours? Great—you are 25 percent complete. We have relied on this method for twenty years, and we know it works well for us. Custom software houses, fabrication job shops, building contractors, and many other industries can use it, too.

The method is not quite as simple as it sounds, however. Do you remember from the previous chapter how we had to estimate remaining COGS expenses and add that to expenses already incurred to get a new total-COGS estimate? It's the same for labor hours. With the Project Management for Profit system, the project manager essentially *reforecasts every week* the hours she anticipates will be necessary to complete the job.

This is another point where the project manager earns her money. Getting an accurate percent-complete figure is one of the toughest tasks she'll undertake. The answer always involves some level of subjectivity. The more you can minimize that subjectivity, the better your chances for a consistent and accurate assessment. Believe us: it's worth the trouble. If a project begins taking on water, you want to know about it as early as possible and be able to take corrective action before things get completely out of control.

Analyzing the Initial Time Report

So again, let's plunge into the nitty-gritty. We'll begin with a simplified example of how the method works. For this example, we'll make the following assumptions about our project:

- Total project revenue $100,000
- Budgeted materials cost $50,000
- Budgeted labor hours   500

Imagine that the project is well under way, and it is time for the project manager to calculate her percent complete. Running the weekly report for labor hours already applied to the project, she finds that her team has logged 300 hours up to this point. Figure 5-1 shows the subtotals for each category. (Just as we did with COGS, we'll limit the number of categories for simplicity's sake.)

FIGURE 5-1

Project #5028 Time Report			
Data from Jan 1 to June 3			
Date	**Task**	**Hours**	**Comment**
June 3	Engineering	120	
June 3	Design	100	
June 3	Mech assembly	40	
June 3	Elect assembly	40	
June 3	Start-up	0	
Total hours for period from Jan 1 to June 3			300

With a budgeted total of 500 labor hours and 300 hours applied so far, you might conclude that the project is 60 percent complete by this measure. Not so fast. That conclusion depends on one crucial assumption—namely, that the project manager estimated total hours with perfect accuracy in the beginning, and so she now needs exactly 200 more labor hours to finish the job. No experienced project manager would make that assumption. To get a better estimate of the remaining hours, the manager must look closely at the remaining tasks on the weekly updated project schedule and estimate the labor hours required to complete them.

So let's look at the labor report in greater detail. Figure 5-2 lists the breakdown of labor hours for the project, including the original bid or budgeted hours, actual hours to date, estimated hours to complete, and total hours projected to finish the job. Note, however, a couple of important provisos about the data in this preliminary figure:

- The project manager has not yet reforecast the hours required. So the "estimated hours to completion" column is calculated by the software. In most cases it is simply bid hours minus actual hours.

- In one case, however—engineering—actual hours are greater than bid hours. The system assumes that there are zero estimated hours to completion, since it can't have a negative number in that column. But check out the "bid hours remaining" column, and note that there is a negative number in the engineering task line. This is the system's acknowledgment that the project exceeded budgeted time for engineering.

As you can see at the bottom of figure 5-2, the software tallies up actual hours and projected hours to give you a percent-complete figure for the overall project. Again: since the project manager has not yet made any adjustments to her hours forecast, it simply indicates a calculated percent complete based upon the original bid hours.

FIGURE 5-2

Project #5028 Hours Calculations				
Task	Bid hrs	Hrs to date	Bid hrs rem	Est hrs comp
Elect assembly	100	40	60	60
Mech assembly	100	40	60	60
Engineering	100	120	(20)	0
Design	100	100	0	0
Start-up	100	0	100	100
Hours totals	**500**	**300**	**200**	**220**

Hours totals	
Forecast total	520
Percentage totals	
Hrs % of bid	104.00%
Hrs % of comp	57.69%

Updated June 3

But it does reflect the labor overrun in the engineering task line. Remember how we said we could make a quick (and probably incorrect) calculation of 60 percent complete based on the 300 hours of actual labor so far? Well, already that assumption has proved false. The engineering task is complete, but it required 120 hours rather than the 100 hours that were in the budget. So the system has calculated that total required hours for the project are now 520, and the percent complete is only 57.69 (300 divided by 520), rather than 60.

Reforecasting Hours

Now it is time for the project manager to estimate how much labor will be required to finish the job. She has only 200 hours left in her budget. Will that be enough? She must scrutinize each outstanding task in detail and project the number of hours she thinks will be necessary to finish up the project.

In this project, the project manager knows that the team has completed both the engineering and design tasks, so she'll project the estimated hours to complete for these tasks at zero.

The two assembly tasks are underway and making good progress, but let's imagine that they are a little more complex than she had originally expected. So she's going to add 15 hours onto each task. That's a better reflection of what she now thinks it will take to finish the tasks. Combining the 15 additional hours with the remaining 60 budgeted hours, she forecasts that each of the assembly tasks will take 75 more hours to complete.

The start-up task, which in a business like Setpoint's might include software and hardware debugging and design refinements, has yet not begun. But now that the project manager knows more about the technology involved, she believes that it will take significantly more effort than originally budgeted. So she adds another 50 hours to that task. Now the projected total is 150 hours, rather than the original budget of 100 hours.

Finally, the project manager enters the required adjustments in the "estimated hours to complete" column (on the right-hand side of figure 5-2).

When this new data hits the system, the software recalculates the project's total hours, overruns, and overall percent complete. And look what it shows! The first thing that jumps out is that the project manager is now projecting a 20 percent overrun in the hours budget. She had 500 budgeted hours to start the job, but now she is forecasting that it will take 600 hours to complete. And since the actual number of hours to date remains unchanged at 300, the calculated percent complete now stands at 50 percent. That's a far cry from the 60 percent number that we first guessed. It's also quite a ways from the 57.69 percent calculation we found before the reforecasting of hours.

FIGURE 5-3

Project #5028 Hours Calculations				
Task	**Bid hrs**	**Hrs to date**	**Bid hrs rem**	**Est hrs comp**
Elect assembly	100	40	60	75
Mech assembly	100	40	60	75
Engineering	100	120	(20)	0
Design	100	100	0	0
Start-up	100	0	100	150
Hours totals	**500**	**300**	**200**	**300**

Hours totals		
Forecast total	600	
Percentage totals		
Hrs % of bid	120.00%	
Hrs % of comp	50.00%	*Updated June 3*

Limitations of the Method

The hours-reforecasting method is likely to give you a far more accurate percent-complete figure than any other method we have come across. But it's a tool, not a magic bullet, and like all tools, it has its limitations. We want to mention three.

Practice Makes Perfect

The first point—and it's a big one—is that the craft of project management will always be an expert system. The more experience you have on the job, the better a project manager you are likely to be. As much as we might like to believe we could build a system that eliminated that need for expertise, we can't. Experienced project managers are far more likely than inexperienced project managers to reforecast their hours accurately.

However, the hours-reforecasting method helps rookies become veterans more quickly. Reforecasting your hours to completion every week is like a crash course in time estimation, and the more you do it, the better you will be. What's more, experienced project managers from your company can help you learn even faster. A company that runs multiple projects is likely to have a few people who are great at reforecasting their hours and who can share their secrets with novices.

Use for Modest-Size Projects

Second, this method of reforecasting hours to determine percent complete works best for projects that require 1,000 hours of labor or less. Once a project gets to be bigger than that, the methodology becomes too complex. Larger projects require an earned value table, which we will take up in chapter 8.

Supplement with Scheduling Software

The best way to estimate labor on projects of 1,000 hours or less is to use a Gantt chart scheduling tool in conjunction with the task list. There are many such tools commercially available. Their features and functionality range from simple timeline illustrators to comprehensive packages that allocate resources and track labor expenses along with their scheduling functions. In our experience, however, the more complex features of these packages don't always work well with the Project Management for Profit system. Some are redundant, and others require more work to construct and maintain than they are worth. For ourselves, we favor Microsoft Project, but we utilize only its task-tracking, scheduling, and Gantt chart features. A big plus in favor of MS Project is that many companies rely on it, so sharing schedules with customers and vendors is pretty easy.

Whatever software you choose, you should always try to keep the tasks that you schedule shorter than two weeks in length. One week is even better. This makes the whole thing more manageable, and it minimizes the impact on the project if a given task is inaccurately analyzed or reported. In general, make sure that the task-tracking and schedule-charting functions of the software are complete and robust. If you can use some of the software's fancier features in your organization, great. But we recommend closely analyzing what you really need before you spend a ton of money. Download demo packages if possible, and try them out in your business before you buy. Most companies offer free trial periods with full functionality for a few weeks or a month.

Now that you understand COGS estimation and labor-hours reforecasting to get an accurate percent-complete figure, it's time to put everything into a functioning system. Beginning with the following chapter, we'll see how all the numbers fit together to help you keep your project on track and on budget.

CHAPTER 5 TAKEAWAYS

- You must manage internal labor as tightly as you manage COGS. Instead of measuring labor *costs,* use labor *hours* as your indicator.

- The worksheet you use must be religiously updated weekly as follows:
  - Hours spent to date.
  - Remaining hours required to complete.

- Hours spent divided by *total* estimated hours to complete (hours spent plus estimated remaining hours). This percentage shows you how far along you are in the project.

• Understand the difference between labor time bid and current total estimated hours to complete in order to take appropriate action.

CHAPTER 6

THE CRITICAL NUMBER: GROSS PROFIT PER HOUR

One of us, Brad, served in a previous life as a navigator on a U.S. Air Force KC-135 Stratotanker. That's where he learned the importance of gauges. Here's his story:

> From day one at flight school our instructors pounded into our heads that relying on our senses to figure out what was going on with our aircraft was not an acceptable aviation practice. In fact, it was a fool's journey that would eventually end in unrecoverable losses of U.S. government property. Mechanical *and* biological losses, they stressed. The instructors backed up their warnings with huge piles of statistics documenting a number of untimely ends to perfectly good USAF airplanes. All of these were directly attributable to one thing: the pilots failed to rely on their instruments and instead used their instincts to tell them what to do with the controls.

At one point the instructors decided to demonstrate how misguided our human senses could be. They were going to put each of us, one at a time, into a specially designed chair that sat inside what looked like a two-axis gyroscope. They would blindfold the subject and then ask him what aerial maneuver he would like to perform—loop, barrel roll, split S, and so on. After that, presumably, we would be run through the simulated maneuver by the twisting and spinning gyro unit. My last name began with A, so I became the first victim of the demonstration.

As I slid into the seat, the instructor directed me to put on the seat belt. That seemed ridiculous at the time—I was sitting in a chair on solid ground, not in an airplane—but I complied. I chose the split S as my maneuver, put on my blindfold, and waited for the adventure to begin.

They leaned me slightly to one side, and then slowly completed several horizontal rotations of the device, getting my inner ear acclimated to the gyrations. So far there hadn't been anything close to vertical—head over heels—rotations. Then, suddenly, they stopped the horizontal rotations and leaned me back up straight. That's when the chaos began. I thought I was being turned upside down and bucked out of the chair. My arms were flailing, trying to grab anything I could to arrest my fall. I was now thankful that I had that seatbelt on.

As my brain started to creep back to its usual moorings, I slowly became aware of the roar of laughter rising from the audience of second lieutenants who were watching. I instantly realized that I had been fooled by my senses. I was still sitting upright in my chair and had never come close to being flipped upside down. But it sure felt that way. I became a believer that very day: we had to rely on our instruments. Instruments don't lie. Senses, instincts, and gut feel lie on a regular basis.

Running a project is something like flying a plane. If you have the right instruments and gauges, your odds of completing a safe and profitable journey increase one hundredfold. You know where you are and in which direction you're headed. You know whether you're in danger of running into an unforeseen source of trouble. (In the flying world, that is known as running into cumulous granite—a mountain.) You know how much leeway you have to make course corrections. And you don't have to rely on your intuition.

This chapter is about creating critical gauges that you need to manage both a project and a project-based company successfully—and to avoid being thrown off track by your senses, instincts, and gut feel.

The Number That Ties Things Together

Think about what you have learned so far. You know how to estimate total COGS from week to week. You know how to estimate a project's percent complete using the labor hours–reforecasting method. These are key parts of the whole. What you need now is a single number that:

- Links the various measures together

- Lets you see at a glance how your project is faring

- Gives you something to share with your team members—a "score" that everyone can understand.

- Enables you to track your performance in any given week as well as the cumulative performance on the entire project to date

In the Project Management for Profit system, that number is gross profit per hour. We'll refer to it here as GP/H.

Properly determined, GP/H reflects the labor hours and materials already invested in the project, along with the hours and materials estimated to complete the project. Every time someone works on a project task, the system recognizes a corresponding portion of the overall project gross profit as "earned." GP/H gives the project manager a dollar-per-hour value for all of this work since the previous week *and* a cumulative value for the hours logged on the project since its inception. Any deviations from the budgeted numbers for labor and materials, positive or negative, show up immediately in the cumulative number.

Let's work through an example, so that the power of this one number becomes clear. We'll assume you're starting a project with revenue of $1 million. The estimated COGS for the job is $600,000, which leaves you with a projected gross profit of $400,000:

$1,000,000	Total project revenue
− 600,000	Projected cost of goods sold (COGS)
$ 400,000	Projected gross profit

The $400,000 in gross profit, of course, must pay for all of your internal labor expenses for the project, for business overhead allocations, for unforeseen budget overruns, and for warranty reserves. You hope that it will also be sufficient to provide your company with a net profit when the accounting is done. In other words, it's a *very* important number.

Now let's look in on this project a month down the road, when it is under way. So far, there have been no surprises, either pleasant or unpleasant. Estimated COGS is exactly as you budgeted it, $600,000, and adjusted gross profit is $400,000. Using the labor-reforecasting method, you determine that the project is 20 percent complete. Last week the completion percentage was 10 percent, so your team finished another 10 percent of the project during the week. In effect, your team *earned* 10 percent of the project's gross profit, or $40,000, that week:

Earned gross profit for week = total gross profit × percent completed that week

And how much effort did it take you to earn it? You check your time report and discover that team members worked 500 hours on the project during the week. Divide the $40,000 by 500 hours and you can see that your team earned $80 of gross profit for each hour invested in the project that week. Your GP/H, in short, is $80 for the week. Here's the full calculation:

$1,000,000	Total project revenue
− 600,000	Cost of goods sold (COGS)
$400,000	Gross profit
× 10%	Completion percentage achieved this week
$ 40,000	Earned gross profit for the week
÷ 500	Hours logged by the project team for the week
$ 80.00	Gross profit per hour earned for the week (GP/H)

To illustrate the impact of a COGS budget overrun on GP/H, let's take that same project and assume some unpleasant surprises. In particular, we'll assume that we got bad news from purchasing, and that the new adjusted COGS is $700,000.

That means we're projecting only $300,000 in gross profit. Now the calculation looks like this:

$300,000	Gross profit
× 10%	Completion percentage achieved this week
$ 30,000	Earned gross profit for the week
÷ 500	Hours logged by the project team for the week
$ 60.00	Gross profit per hour for the week (GP/H)

The $100,000 change in COGS leads to a decrease in GP/H of $20 an hour for the week. In effect, $100,000 of project revenue has moved from the gross profit category over to the COGS category, and all of your gross profit metrics take a hit, including your GP/H.

(If you had been pleasantly instead of unpleasantly surprised —if your COGS were to come in $100,000 *under* your projected budget, for example—that saving would also shift your total gross profit, increasing it to $500,000. As an exercise, calculate what your GP/H for the week would have been, using the same assumptions.)

Cumulative and Weekly GP/H

You can see that it is equally easy to calculate total GP/H for the life of a project to date. All you do is use your most current projected gross profit multiplied by your total percent complete to date and then divided by total hours.

This cumulative number is really the most important number to watch, especially as you close in on the end of a project. It tells you how you have done throughout the project's life, good weeks and bad averaged together. It's a handy indicator of where your project's overall finances really stand. Weekly GP/H numbers tend to rise and fall a little; they get bumped around by the usual issues that crop up in any project.

But the cumulative total should stay pretty consistent. Changes in this number do occur, for both the good and the bad, but the change is seldom dramatic from one week to another. In fact, if cumulative GP/H does change dramatically in a short period of time, it's probably a result of tracking or reporting errors rather than actual project issues.

But let's imagine for the moment that some sort of disaster has occurred—maybe like the invoice that Mike the excavator received from his subcontractor (see chapter 3). Last week you knew nothing of it; this week it is all too apparent, and you have to take the entire hit in one bite. The pain involved in this sort of correction is twofold. There's an immediate impact on your week's earned gross profit, which will surely turn out negative. Your project's cumulative GP/H will also reflect the hit: it will drop by a commensurate amount. In essence, you have to give money back on all the hours previously worked on the project. It's probably not a good day to be that project's manager. Our experience tells us that bad news does not get better with time. As a general rule, *whenever you know accurate information, good or bad, put it into the system.*

This simple GP/H scorekeeping methodology makes it easy to quantify the financial success of project teams every week. Over time, you will be able to set benchmarks for acceptable and unacceptable levels of GP/H. What an acceptable number is, of course, depends on your business. (At Setpoint, we regard anything less than $80 as cause for concern, unless it's really only temporary.) So long as your projects remain above that number, you know you're doing OK. If GP/H begins to head downward—and particularly if it heads downward for more than a week or two—you know not only that you have problems but also what the magnitude of the problems is. That's when you dig down into your COGS figures and your labor hours to determine where the problems lie and what you can do about them.

Given an accurate percent-complete estimate, the Project Management for Profit system quickly calculates what each team earns in gross profit dollars for every hour. Assuming that the data is fresh, this provides you with something very close to a real-time system of reporting. *You now know the score.* You can see every week exactly how your project teams are doing, and you can identify and mitigate financial issues right then, rather than just looking at whether you won or lost after the project is over. That by itself is a game changer, and it's all wrapped up in one simple number, GP/H.

From Project Profitability to Company Profitability

GP/H is a measure of the profitability of any given project. That's a key number for any project-based company, because if the projects don't make money, then the company doesn't make money. But a company is more than just an individual project. How can you be sure that *all* the projects are generating enough gross profit to support the business? Project Management for Profit incorporates two additional metrics that will help keep your company in the black.

GP/OE

One useful measure is a simple ratio: earned gross profit during a given period of time divided by the company's overall operating expenses (OE or SG&A) for the same period. For example, a GP/OE metric of 1.25 tells you that you generated 25 percent more gross profit than the business spent on operating expenses for a given period. We recommend that you calculate the ratio weekly, so that you can be sure it stays in the right zone.

What the right zone is, again, depends on your business. But the ratio obviously should be as high as possible, and in our experience it should definitely be higher than about 1.2. If it begins to creep toward 1.0—or, worse, if it sinks below 1.0—something is amiss in the company's efficiency. There's not enough gross profit to support the business; or, to view the matter from the other direction, operating expenses are too high for the amount of gross profit your projects are generating.

GP/OE is likely to be one of the numbers you watch most closely. If you share numbers with employees, as Setpoint does, you'll find that nearly everyone monitors and discusses it. It's a quick and tidy indicator of whether the business as a whole is winning or losing.

Percent Direct

The *percent direct* figure is the percentage of overall company labor that is directly charged to projects that generate gross profit. Recorded weekly, it's a measure of how many employee hours were actually earning gross profit compared to how many were charged to overhead activities. Most project managers have had firsthand experience with companies that slowly transformed themselves into top-heavy albatrosses without even realizing it. This metric can help you make sure that doesn't happen.

Tracking percent direct enables you to scrutinize and justify overhead expenses every week, rather than allowing those expenses to creep up and quietly devour the company's net profits. It helps you keep the company lean. Direct labor is the breadwinner, and you need to keep the right balance between direct labor and support activities. Loss of control in this area can have a negative effect on just about any company, but it can crush a small company quickly.

OK. Right about now, you may be thinking something like this: "Holy cow, that's an incredible amount of information to gather, record, and calculate just to track a project's financial status. I'm not sure I can do all that—and anyway, where will I find the time?" Don't give up! The Project Management for Profit approach is expressly designed to make the information-gathering process friendly and systematic. In the following chapter, we'll introduce the tool that makes all this tracking and calculation possible.

CHAPTER 6 TAKEAWAYS

- Gross profit per hour (GP/H) is the key metric to understand and know how to calculate. This critical number tells you how much your project has earned for the current week.

- The key calculation looks like this:

	Revenue for project
−	Latest COGS worksheet total (chapter 4)
=	Gross profit for project
×	% complete achieved for week
=	Earned gross profit for week
÷	Hours logged by project team
=	Gross profit per hour (GP/H) for the week

CHAPTER 7

THE GROSS PROFIT PER HOUR WORKSHEET

Most project-based companies aren't made up of accountants. In fact, a lot of project managers—contractors, engineers, marketers, whatever they may be—have little background in accounting or finance. So tracking the financial status of a project has to be easy. It shouldn't require any financial expertise.

Then, too, nobody can afford to spend half the workweek hovering over a calculator to figure out how a project is faring. The legwork of tracking and calculating a project's financial status has to be just a small part of the project manager's weekly routine.

Our conclusion? Every project manager needs a simple tool—a scoreboard or dashboard—that lets him calculate and see exactly where things stand, with as little effort as possible. In the Project Management for Profit system, this tool is the *gross profit per hour worksheet*, or just the GP/H worksheet.

The GP/H worksheet will keep you apprised of your successes and failures—quickly, accurately, and regularly. All you need to do is update a few fields, and you will see your GP/H for the previous week and the overall financial status of the project to date.

There are just three sets of numbers you must update on a weekly basis to keep your project current:

- Total project COGS expense, including both completed expenditures and any estimated costs to complete

- Hours applied to the project for the week

- The percent complete of the project

Pull these up, plug them in, and your project score will materialize right before your eyes. As we'll see, you can also use the worksheet to forecast where you are likely to be in future periods—an invaluable piece of information for any project manager.

Using the GP/H Worksheet

Figure 7-1 is a sample GP/H worksheet. Since it is on a computer, it may look complicated. It isn't. We'll dissect it—and show you how to use it—in three easy steps.

To get started, let's construct a GP/H worksheet piece by piece for a sample project. We'll use the following bid numbers for the sake of simplicity:

Total project revenue	$100,000
Budgeted materials cost	$ 50,000
Budgeted labor hours	500 hours

FIGURE 7-1

Setpoint GP/H Worksheet

	Last	May	June													Bid
Proj	Month % comp	Fct % comp	Fct % comp	Prev % comp	Current % comp	Project revenue	Bid COGS	Actual COGS	Project GP	Earned GP	Previous GP	Week GP	Week hours	Week GP/HR	To-date GP/HR	GP/HR
5555.00	0.00%	0.00%	0.00%	0.00%	0.00%	$100,000	$50,000	$50,000	$50,000	$0	$0	$0	0			$100

Totals

	Week 1	Week 2	Week 3	Week 4
# of days	5	5	5	5

Week GP					
Actual	$0	$0	$0	$0
Forecast	$0	$0	$0	$0
B/W	$0	$0	$0	$0

MTD GP					
Actual	$0	$0	$0	$0
Forecast	$0	$0	$0	$0
B/W	$0	$0	$0	$0

Hours to date

Proj	To-date hours	Bid GP	Bid hours
5555.00	0.00	$50,000	500.00

Forecast (% Increase per month)

	May		June	
Proj	%	GP	%	GP
5555.00	0.00%	$0	0.00%	$0
	Total GP		Total GP	

Month forecast   <-- Manually enter month forecast

The project manager enters these numbers in the corresponding fields at the start of the project. The worksheet's formulas calculate total budgeted gross profit (see figure 7-2).

FIGURE 7-2

Project revenue	Bid COGS	Actual COGS	Project GP
$100,000	$50,000	$50,000	$50,000

At this point, of course, actual COGS matches bid COGS because we are just beginning the project.

Next, the project manager enters budgeted hours for the project (see figure 7-3).

FIGURE 7-3

Proj	To-date hours	Bid GP	Bid hours
5555.00	0.00	$50,000	500.00

The worksheet calculates the project's bid GP/H by dividing projected total gross profit by the number of budgeted hours. The bid gross profit per hour is what the company is expecting to make on the project (see figure 7-4). That figure never changes; it is used purely as a benchmark to compare ongoing results with the original projections.

FIGURE 7-4

Week hours	Week GP/HR	To-date GP/HR	Bid GP/HR
0.00			$100

These are the entries at the beginning of the project—the starting point. Now let's see how to use the worksheet on an ongoing basis.

Step 1: COGS

It's Monday, and the project manager is reviewing where things stand. Like most good project managers, he likes to see weekly updates rather than monthly ones. We'll assume that our project was 50 percent complete at the beginning of last week. This will let us illustrate some of the issues that arise as a project is in full swing.

First, the project manager runs a report on his project's COGS expenses to date. Then he recalculates his COGS estimated-to-complete numbers and enters them in the worksheet.

As it happens, last week was a rough week for the COGS budget. One of the major materials suppliers raised its prices because of a surge in demand from China. With the new pricing now known, it's obvious the project is going to exceed its budget, and the numbers the manager enters will reflect this fact.

The system totals COGS expenditures incurred to date plus the project manager's new forecast of COGS estimate-to-completion. This sum is the "actual COGS" total that he will enter on his GP/H worksheet (see figure 7-5). As you can see, the project has already incurred $54,500 in COGS expenditures, and the project manager is now estimating that he'll need an additional $3,000 to finish the job. So total COGS for this project now sits at $57,500, even though the bid COGS budget was only $50,000. As a result, the project's total gross profit is going to take a $7,500 hit this week.

FIGURE 7-5

COGS Review Report							
Project - 5555			Customer - Sample			Report date - June 3	
Category	Bid $	Actual $	$ Remain in bid	Est $ to comp	Project % comp	% of bid	Total
Electric	$25,000	$23,500	$1,500	$2,500	90.38%	94.00%	$26,000
Fabricated	$25,000	$31,000	($6,000)	$500	98.41%	124.00%	$31,500
Totals	$50,000	$54,500	($4,500)	$3,000	94.78%	115.00%	$57,500

Before we ask the project manager to enter the new COGS total on his GP/H worksheet, let's take a quick look at the gross profit metrics for the project as they were *beforehand* (see figure 7-6).

FIGURE 7-6

Project revenue	Bid COGS	Actual COGS	Project GP	Earned GP	Previous GP
$100,000	$50,000	$50,000	$50,000	$25,000	$25,000

Now he enters the new figures for COGS. As expected, overall project gross profit drops by the corresponding amount of the COGS overrun (see figure 7-7).

FIGURE 7-7

Project revenue	Bid COGS	Actual COGS	Project GP	Earned GP	Previous GP
$100,000	$50,000	$57,500	$42,500	$21,250	$25,000

Remember that we're assuming the project was 50 percent complete at the start of the week, so *earned* gross profit is half of total project gross profit. Note an important fact that the worksheet shows: the project's earned gross profit has now decreased from \$25,000 to \$21,250 because of the decrease in total gross profit. The project manager has to "give back" \$3,750 in gross profit that he had previously claimed as earned to make up for the impact of the budget overrun. (He doesn't have to give back the full \$7,500 in COGS overrun because the project is only 50 percent complete.)

For any project, a comparison of actual COGS to bid COGS is a key measure. If COGS is significantly over budget, there may be a change order lurking in there somewhere. Scope creep can't hide in this system, as the effects of change orders show up immediately. Large discrepancies here can also identify issues with a project's execution or a shortcoming on the job's original bid. Whatever the cause, you are at least dragging the problem out into the sunshine. That lets you take corrective steps as early as possible. It also helps you learn where you can do better on future projects.

Step 2: Hours and Percent Complete

The project manager then runs the project's weekly and cumulative hours reports from the database. In this example, let's say he learns that his team put in 50 hours last week on the project, for a cumulative total of 300 hours to date (see figures 7-8 and 7-9). (See chapter 5 for a refresher if necessary.)

The project manager now enters the hours figures in the appropriate fields on his GP/H worksheet (see figures 7-10 and 7-11).

Once the earned gross profit for the week is tallied and entered, these hours entries will be used to calculate GP/H, both for the week and for the project overall.

Now comes the big number: the project's percent-complete calculation.

In this example we'll assume that the forecast hours for the project haven't changed since the beginning of the project.

FIGURE 7-8

Project #5555 Time Report			
Data from June 5 to June 11			
Date	**Task**	**Hours**	**Comment**
June 11	Mech assembly	25	
June 11	Elect assembly	25	
Total hours for period from June 5 to June 11			50

FIGURE 7-9

Project #5555 Time Report			
Data from Jan 1 to June 11			
Date	**Task**	**Hours**	**Comment**
June 11	Engineering	100	
June 11	Design	100	
June 11	Mech assembly	50	
June 11	Elect assembly	50	
Total hours for period from Jan 1 to June 11			300

FIGURE 7-10

Week GP	Week hours	Week GP/HR	To-date GP/HR	Bid GP/HR
$0.00	50.00		$100.00	$100.00

FIGURE 7-11

Proj	To-date hours	Bid GP	Bid hours
5555.00	300.00	$50,000	500.00

We're making this assumption purely for the sake of simplicity; in reality, projected hours would probably have been adjusted a number of times by now. So prior to the week we're looking at, the team had logged 250 hours against a forecast of 500 hours. The project was 50 percent complete, and it had earned 50 percent of total gross profit.

Now let's look at the project status report page for the end of the week *before* any changes are made to the estimated-to-complete fields. It shows 300 hours already logged: the 250 from prior weeks and the 50 from the week just ended. Since our budget is 500 hours, the report shows we are 60 percent complete (see figure 7-12).

FIGURE 7-12

Project #5555 Hours Calculations				
Task	**Bid hrs**	**Hrs to date**	**Bid hrs rem**	**Est hrs comp**
Elect assembly	100	50	50	50
Mech assembly	100	50	50	50
Engineering	100	100	0	0
Design	100	100	0	0
Start-up	100	0	100	100
Hours totals	**500**	**300**	**200**	**200**
Hours totals				
Forecast total	500			
Percentage totals				
Hrs % of bid	100.00%			
Hrs % of comp	60.00%			*Updated June 11*

But last week was a week of bad news. Not only did COGS go up, but the project manager learned of several problems that cropped up during the assembly phase of the project. He now needs to make some adjustments to his forecast hours in order to determine his completion percentage accurately. Going back to the project's hours database, he adjusts the estimated hours to complete in each of the two assembly categories from 50 to 75. That reflects the additional hours he now expects will be required to finish the tasks (see figure 7-13).

FIGURE 7-13

Project #5555 Hours Calculations				
Task	**Bid hrs**	**Hrs to date**	**Bid hrs rem**	**Est hrs comp**
Elect assembly	100	50	50	75
Mech assembly	100	50	50	75
Engineering	100	100	0	0
Design	100	100	0	0
Start-up	100	0	100	100
Hours totals	**500**	**300**	**200**	**250**

Hours totals			
Forecast total	550		
Percentage totals			
Hrs % of bid	110.00%		
Hrs % of comp	54.55%		*Updated June 11*

We can see from figure 7-13 that the project's overall completion percentage has now decreased from 60 percent to 54.55 percent. The report also shows that he is estimating a 10 percent overrun in the project's hours budget. So the project manager will enter 54.55 percent as the completion percentage in the GP/H worksheet (see figure 7-14).

FIGURE 7-14

Current % comp	Prev % comp	Project revenue	Bid COGS	Actual COGS	Project GP
54.55%	50.00%	$100,000	$50,000	$57,500	$42,500

Once the percent-complete number is entered in the proper field, the worksheet calculates the percentage earned for the week simply by subtracting the previous week's earned percentage. In this case that calculation is simple:

54.55% – 50.00% = 4.55%.

The worksheet then calculates the amount of gross profit earned for the week by multiplying that percentage by total project gross profit.

Before you look at the outcome of all this, you'll want to remind yourself of the two important facts that brought the project to this point:

1. The project manager added $7,500 to the COGS budget, thereby reducing the project's total gross profit by that much.

2. He also added 50 more hours, or 10 percent, to the project labor budget.

Either of these actions on its own can make a pretty big dent in a project's weekly finances. Together, they usually spell big trouble.

How big is the trouble in this case? Let's look at the week's earned gross profit on the worksheet. It shows that everything that happened during the week resulted in a *negative* earned gross profit of $1,816 for the week. That translates into –$36.32 GP/H for every hour logged on the project in that week (see figure 7-15).

FIGURE 7-15

Project revenue	Bid COGS	Actual COGS	Project GP	Earned GP	Previous GP	Week GP	Week hours	Week GP/HR	To-date GP/HR
$100,000	$50,000	$57,500	$42,500	$23,184	$25,000	($1,816)	50.00	($36.33)	$77.28

You can also see that the project's cumulative GP/H has now dipped to $77.28 from the bid number of $100 per hour. Ouch.

After the project manager has entered all of this data, the project's updated GP/H worksheet now looks like what is shown in figures 7-16 and 7-17.

FIGURE 7-16

Proj	Last Month % comp	May Fct % comp	June Fct % comp	Current % comp	Prev % comp	Project revenue	Bid COGS	Actual COGS
5555.00	0.00%	0.00%	0.00%	54.55%	50.00%	$100,000	$50,000	$57,500

FIGURE 7-17

Project GP	Earned GP	Previous GP	Week GP	Week hours	Week GP/HR	To-date GP/HR	Bid GP/HR
$42,500	$23,184	$25,000	($1,816)	50.00	($36.33)	$77.28	$100.00

If the whole company is working on this system, the project manager now gives his updated GP/H worksheet to the accounting department, which adds up the worksheets from all of the company's project teams. The accountants then combine that data with operating expenses so they can quickly see how the company did financially for the week. Looking at the cumulative numbers, they can also get a quick read on financial performance for the month, quarter, or year to date.

If this were your project, think about what you would be learning about its status just by looking at the GP/H worksheet:

- You did earn some gross profit from this project last week, just not enough to cover the dramatic corrections to the estimated-to-complete numbers. That's the reason for the negative GP/H figure. What you have really determined is that you had previously claimed more gross profit than you were entitled to. Now you have to pay it all back, so to speak, to square things up with the "bank."

- The specific issues that led to the COGS and hours overruns may already be beyond the help of any corrective actions, but at least you know about them relatively early in the project. And since you know the dollar value of both problems, you and your team can be more vigilant going forward. You can also look harder for creative solutions in other areas of the project that might offset the overruns. Knowledge is power, particularly for a project manager.

Most real-world projects don't reflect such abrupt negative news. Usually the project manager would have been making adjustments every week. While he may wind up at the same point, the journey would show a gradual downward curve in GP/H rather than the nearly 23 percent drop shown in this example. But crazy things sometimes happen. By calculating and reporting the project earnings weekly, a project manager can identify and address small problems before they can grow into big problems. In this game, big almost always means expensive.

What About Good News?

While the preceding example is all negative, it's important to remember that positive events happen as well. We've seen it often over the years. For example, COGS costs might drop because prices decline. A team might come up with an idea that allows hours, COGS dollars, or both to be removed from the budget. The resulting gains are of course transferred to the project's total gross profit, and GP/H goes up. In most cases, such gains translate directly to that most important number-of-all-numbers, the project's net profit. Good news not only gives you a better GP/H for the week, it also increases the cumulative GP/H of the entire project.

One note of caution: as we noted in an earlier chapter, you have to be careful about realizing budget gains in the middle of a project. Make sure that you have solid facts to back up your actions so you don't have to give gross profit back should your actual gains turn out lower. By the same token, don't just leave your numbers as they are until the end of the project and then realize a huge gain in one chunk. The name for that particular transgression is sandbagging, and nobody likes a sandbagger. We'll have more to say on sandbagging in the following chapter.

Step 3: Forecasting

The GP/H worksheet makes it easier to calculate forecasts for earned gross profit through the remaining months of a project. The same metrics used to calculate earned gross profit to date can be combined with scheduled milestones, hours estimates, and available resources to forecast the future. Such forecasts are great for the accounting department, customers, senior managers, and bankers—they let everyone see how the project manager expects things to unfold in the coming months. The forecasts help the project manager as well, because they instantly highlight potential delays and overruns.

Figure 7-18 shows a GP/H worksheet with the forecasting fields highlighted.

FIGURE 7-18

Alpha Team Board

Proj	Ship date	Last Month % comp	May Fct % comp	June Fct % comp	Project revenue	Prev % comp	Current % comp	Bid COGS	Actual COGS	Project GP	Earned GP	Previous GP	Week GP	Week hours	Week GP/HR	To-date GP/HR	Bid GP/HR
2221.01	Oct 1	50.00%	70.00%	90.00%	$3,500,000	52.15%	60.00%	$2,550,000	$2,500,000	$1,000,000	$600,000	$550,000	$50,000	375.00	$133.33	$109.08	$118.31
2134.00	Dec 1	5.00%	20.00%	30.00%	$3,647,258	0.00%	10.00%	$3,210,609	$3,210,609	$436,649	$43,665	$21,750	$21,915	225.00	$97.40	$174.31	$153.21
												Totals	$71,915	600.00	$119.86		

Forecast (% increase per month)

Proj	May %	May GP	June %	June GP
2221.01	20.00%	$200,000	20.00%	$200,000
2134.00	15.00%	$65,497	10.00%	$43,665
	Total GP	$265,497	Total GP	$243,665

Hours to date

Proj	To-date hours	Bid GP	Bid hours
2221.01	5,500.75	$950,000	8,030
2134.00	250.50	$436,649	2,850

	# of days	Week 1	Week 2	Week 3	Week 4	
		5	5	5	5	
Week GP	Actual	$71,915				
	Forecast	$66,374	$66,374	$66,374	$66,374	$0
	B/W	$5,541	($66,374)	($66,374)	($66,374)	$0
MTD GP	Actual	$71,915	$71,914	$71,914	$71,914	$71,914
	Forecast	$66,374	$132,749	$199,123	$265,497	$265,497
	B/W	$5,541	($60,835)	($127,209)	($193,583)	($193,583)

Month forecast **$265,497**   <-- Manually enter month forecast

The formula for forecasting is simple. The project manager records his project's completion percentage at the start of a month, along with the percentage that he expects to complete in each of the two upcoming months. The system uses those percentages, along with current estimated total gross profit, to calculate the gross profit dollars that the team will earn in each of the coming months (see the right side of figure 7-18). The sample worksheet in figure 7-19 shows that the gross profit forecast for two projects is $265,497 in May and $243,665 in June.

FIGURE 7-19

Forecast (% increase per month)				
	May		June	
Proj	%	GP	%	GP
2221.01	20.00%	$200,000	20.00%	$200,000
2134.00	15.00%	$65,497	10.00%	$43,665
	Total GP	$265,497	**Total GP**	$243,665

To break things down still further, the system takes the forecast gross profit for the current month and plugs it into the earnings section of the GP/H worksheet, where it is divided up into weekly earnings goals (see figure 7-20).

Project managers who use the Project Management for Profit system improve their forecasting skills quickly. When you see forecasts virtually every week and compare them to results, you tend to learn fast. Sometimes new project managers try to sandbag a little at the beginning, plugging in conservative numbers rather than their best estimates. But veterans focus on making their gross profit forecasts every bit as accurate as their earnings calculations, whether the news is good or bad. A company that has accurate forecasts is a thing of beauty. Accountants can

FIGURE 7-20

		Week 1	Week 2	Week 3	Week 4	
	# of days	5	5	5	5	
Week GP	Actual	**$71,915**				
	Forecast	$66,374	$66,374	$66,374	$66,374	$0
	B/W	$5,541	($66,374)	($66,374)	($66,374)	$0
MTD GP	Actual	$71,915	$71,914	$71,914	$71,914	$71,914
	Forecast	$66,374	$132,749	$199,123	$265,497	$265,497
	B/W	$5,541	($60,835)	($127,209)	($193,583)	($193,583)
	Month forecast	**$265,497**	<-- Manually enter month forecast			

estimate the entire company's income statement for months to come. A project-based business using conventional accounting can't do that.

While our sample GP/H worksheets in this chapter show only one project, it's common for many project managers to have several projects running at one time, with all of them listed on the same worksheet. The worksheet can include calculations that total up earnings from multiple projects and create cumulative scores encapsulating all of the manager's projects.

We think you'll find that the GP/H worksheet is a great method for gathering and crunching the data you need to report on a project's progress and calculate the financial score. It's a cornerstone tool of the entire Project Management for Profit system. But before we go on, we'd better take up one vexing subject: what do you do when you have a project too big for accurate hours-to-complete estimates? Do you have to throw out the whole thing?

The answer involves another story.

CHAPTER 7 TAKEAWAYS

- The gross profit per hour worksheet tool has three key functions in the Project Management for Profit system:

  1. It tracks weekly project gross profit.

  2. It tracks cumulative project gross profit.

  3. It helps you forecast future project gross profit.

CHAPTER 8

MANAGING BIG PROJECTS

Remember Setpoint? It's the company that gave birth to the Project Management for Profit system. We told some of the Setpoint story in this book's early chapters. Founders Joe Cornwell and Joe VanDenBerghe had left Arrow, the troubled roller-coaster company, to start their new venture. At first, they vowed to steer clear of the treacherous roller-coaster business. Companies in that industry always seemed to be going broke, just like Arrow.

There was only one problem: Cornwell and VanDenBerghe happened to be particularly good at roller-coaster design and engineering. Though no longer in the industry, they were regularly approached by major amusement parks to consult on design reviews for ongoing projects. The parks also invited Setpoint to bid on building whole rides. Cornwell and VanDenBerghe did some reviews, but they always declined the opportunity to bid on a complete ride. In their view, Setpoint just wasn't big enough to take on such a project.

At one point, though, Universal Studios asked the pair to undertake several third-party design reviews for rides planned for a new park in Orlando, Florida. The park was to be called Universal Studios–Islands of Adventure. Universal must have been happy with the reviews, because a few months later the company called Setpoint with yet another opportunity. The small company that had been building a ride called the Pteranodon Flyer had—guess what—gone out of business. Universal asked Cornwell whether Setpoint would consider finishing the project. This time, after consulting his colleagues, Cornwell said yes.

The decision was a little like a small home-building company agreeing to build a shopping mall. The Pteranodon Flyer was a multimillion-dollar project, five times as big as anything Setpoint had done before. It would require an estimated 15,000 hours of labor. Cornwell, VanDenBerghe, and Joe Knight—the Joes—had to wonder whether the project management system they had been creating at Setpoint would be up to the job.

Big Projects and Blobs

Big projects are different from smaller ones. It isn't just that they involve more moving parts. The real difference has to do with the limitations of the human mind.

Experienced project managers can get their minds around smaller projects. They have an intuitive sense of how to build a house, launch a modest-size ad campaign, create a simple piece of software. To be sure, the numbers—the financial-tracking scores produced by the Project Management for Profit system—are an indispensable check on this gut-level understanding. Like a pilot's instruments, they prevent the project manager from relying too heavily on her instincts and experience, and they tell her in black and white exactly where things stand at any given moment. Still, the experienced project manager is likely to have a pretty good intuitive idea of her progress and her challenges, so long as the project remains relatively small.

With big projects, the experience is different. Setpoint's roller-coaster project, for example, would span eighteen months. It would involve dozens of subcontractors, hundreds of milestones, thousands of tasks and subtasks, and millions of dollars in materials and labor to keep track of. No mere human could hope to monitor such a project by intuition and gut feel.

Simple systems such as Setpoint's original software don't necessarily work well either. The reason is that there are too many undifferentiated tasks, which we will refer to by their scientific name: *blobs.* A blob is a large task or series of tasks required for the project, but with details that are poorly defined and hence poorly understood. If the project manager's task list for that shopping mall had a line that read, "Assemble all necessary materials," that would be a blob.

Blobs typically show up in two guises. One is the large, complex task that is to be performed by a subcontractor. As project manager, you're depending on that subcontractor to complete the job on time and on budget. Yet you have no real idea of how the subcontracting company plans to go about its work, and you don't really know whether your on-time-and-on-budget expectations are reasonable. All you have is one line on your budget that reads something like "Task X: ABC Contracting." Any project-tracking system depends on close monitoring of progress, but with a blob like this, you have none of the detail that you need for effective tracking.

The other kind of blob is a large, undifferentiated block of hours. When you compile a Gantt chart for your project, you may find that you have several long-duration tasks, with hundreds or even thousands of hours devoted to each one, that include few, if any, subtasks or milestones. This was a particular problem for Setpoint's original system. After all, the whole thing depended on accurate forecasting of hours and accurate determination of percent complete. But who can accurately forecast a large labor category that has no subtasks or milestones? You might know that people are working hard on this task, but you have no real way of gauging their progress or reforecasting their likely time to complete.

Let's look at how Setpoint solved these two problems.

Managing Subcontractors

There's no way around this one: whenever a subcontractor is responsible for a large, essential piece of a project, you as project manager have to know exactly what's going on. You don't need to manage the task as if it were your own—it's not—but you need a detailed view into how the subcontractor plans to manage it.

Several years ago, one of the authors of this book, Roger, was managing a Setpoint project. The following story comes from that experience. Only the names have been changed.

> The project we were working on was a complicated new materials-handling system for a manufacturing facility. One portion of the job was a stand-alone subsystem that could be designed and built independently, with only a little collaboration on our part. We decided to outsource it to a subcontractor. The company we had in mind, Quantum Robotics, had a window available. Quantum was a small shop with a talented group of technical people, and it had a reputation for first-class work.
>
> As the project got under way, though, things started to get complicated. We got contradictory directions from

different customer representatives. We had to discard some already-fabricated parts due to bad information. We were facing long delays. Some of the changes would be paid for by the customer, some by Quantum, and some by Setpoint. It was tough enough just trying to track all the changes. But I was also worried that the project would become a financial loser for Quantum. Whenever you rely on a small subcontractor, you have to be concerned about the job's profitability. If the sub takes a big financial hit, it can be blasted right out of existence.

So on one of my regular visits to the Quantum shop I pulled aside Dave, the owner and president, and asked him how his company was doing financially on this project. Dave was a good friend, so I was surprised when he seemed taken aback by my question. "Well, I'm sure we've lost some profit, but I think we're doing OK," he said. He was polite, but he didn't want to discuss it further. Eventually, the reason dawned on me: he didn't know the answer to my question.

Later that day, I broached the subject again, noting that I just wanted to make sure we all made money on the job. Dave pondered for a moment before replying. "We all have the same goal on that point, no question. But honestly, I'm not going to know how profitable this project is for us until we're done with it and we can add up all the final numbers. How profitable is it right now? I'm really not sure. How could I be?" My hunch was right: Dave would have to wait for a final accounting to know the project's profitability.

I returned to my office feeling frustrated. I had grown accustomed to the steady flow of financial data at Setpoint, and I felt helpless without similar scores for Quantum's piece of the project. Wait and see? That was unacceptable—too much was at stake.

The next day, I called Dave and asked whether I could stop by and discuss the project with him. "Did you forget something, or are you just coming back for the free coffee?" he asked, only half-jokingly. Once there, I explained I was still concerned about the financial state of the project, and that I didn't want to lie awake nights worrying about it. A quick shadow crossed Dave's face. "We discussed this subject yesterday. I told you, I won't know how big the impact is until we complete the job and tally up the numbers."

I decided to forge ahead. "Dave, listen," I said. "If you're open to trying something new, I can help you get a better idea of where you stand right now on this project's finances. If you can get me a few pieces of data on the labor and expenses that you've put into the project up to now, I think we can quantify your progress with dollar signs." Dave was scowling, but he agreed. "Come back at three this afternoon," he said, "and we'll see what kind of voodoo you have up your sleeve."

Dave and I met at his office later that day and crunched through all of his project budget and expenditures data. We recorded the hours and dollars already invested. We created and refined detailed forecasts on hours and COGS, and we analyzed percent complete. We calculated his GP/H, both budgeted and actual. Before we went home that night, Dave had a pretty good idea of exactly where he stood financially on this project. And it wasn't terrible—yet. Despite the delays, he was maintaining a reasonable profit. But we identified some areas of concern, things that could turn into expensive problems. Dave wrote those issues on the whiteboard in his office and underlined them boldly. "If we can keep these issues in check, this will work out to be a profitable project. We'll watch them closely from here on out. And we'll be tracking our GP/H numbers on a regular basis, too." He and I were both relieved to know where things stood. And Dave now had the tools to continue tracking the project all the way to the finish line.

Three weeks later, I was back at Quantum for another progress visit. Our walk-through revealed that his team had made up some significant time. So I asked the obvious question: "With all this progress in such a short period, your GP/H must have jumped up significantly. Where did all this good news push your numbers to?" Dave got a deer-in-the-headlights look. "Um, that's a great question. We should sit down and figure that out." I found out later that he hadn't even looked at any of the project financial data since our first session weeks ago.

"We talked about continuing to track progress on the GP/H for the rest of the job," I said. "Why didn't you follow through on that?"

"Well, once things were going better, it didn't seem to be as critical," Dave replied. "We're doing great now, I bet!"

I sighed and rolled my eyes. This was not going to be easy. Once again I walked Dave through the numbers. We compiled his GP/H for the last few weeks and for the project overall. The results were surprising to me and unbelievable to Dave. While there was a modest improvement, it was not nearly as large as

Dave and I had expected it to be. A close analysis of the data showed why. The progress over the last few weeks was impressive, but it came at a price. The team had worked a significant amount of extra hours, and Dave had underestimated the impact of those hours on his bottom line. After about three trips through the numbers, he finally believed what he saw in front of him.

"OK, I get it," he said. "I can see the value of tracking the metrics that you use. We'll run the numbers every week for the life of the project so we can stay on top of things. Thanks for taking the time to share your system with us."

Managing subcontractors in this way can be difficult and time-consuming. But allowing such a blob to dictate the outcome of your project is usually an unacceptable risk. If you divide the blobs up into agreed-on subtasks and milestones, you and your subcontractors can accurately track progress, identify issues more quickly, and ultimately turn in better performance. If you introduce them to the Project Management for Profit system, you can get the same information from them that you get from your own projects.

Don't fall victim to the hope-and-a-prayer approach to project management, hoping and praying that the subcontractor will deliver the right goods at the right time. It's your project, and you have to know where things stand at all times.

The Problem of Managing Hours

Managing your own team's hours is a different matter entirely. For this, you'll need a tool called an *earned value table*.

First let's take a little closer look at the details of the problem. We'll go through a simplified example to illustrate the shortcoming of the original Setpoint system when it was applied to such a big project.

Figure 8-1 shows a simplified project-hours worksheet for a 15,000-hour roller-coaster project.

You can see in the sample project-hours report that we have broken the 15,000 hours down into five labor categories, budgeted at 3,000 hours each.

Now the project gets rolling, and we're ready to do our first weekly analysis of the project's completion percentage so that we can calculate earned gross profit and GP/H. The project manager runs his updated hours report and notes that his team has logged a total of 250 hours on the project to date (see figure 8-2). The hours logged against the project span three different labor categories; two categories as yet have no hours.

FIGURE 8-1

Project #6307 Hours Calculations				
Task	**Bid hrs**	**Hrs to date**	**Bid hrs rem**	**Est hrs comp**
Elect assembly	3,000		3,000	3,000
Mech assembly	3,000		3,000	3,000
Engineering	3,000		3,000	3,000
Design	3,000		3,000	3,000
Installation	3,000		3,000	3,000
Hours totals	**15,000**	**0**	**15,000**	**15,000**

Hours totals			
Forecast total	15,000		
Percentage totals			
Hrs % of bid	100.00%		
Hrs % of comp	0.00%		*Updated June 11*

FIGURE 8-2

Project #6307 Hours Calculations				
Task	**Bid hrs**	**Hrs to date**	**Bid hrs rem**	**Est hrs comp**
Elect assembly	3,000		3,000	3,000
Mech assembly	3,000	25	2,975	2,975
Engineering	3,000	150	2,850	2,850
Design	3,000	75	2,925	2,925
Installation	3,000		3,000	3,000
Hours totals	**15,000**	**250**	**14,750**	**14,750**

Hours totals			
Forecast total	15,000		
Percentage totals			
Hrs % of bid	100.00%		
Hrs % of comp	1.67%		*Updated June 11*

As you can see from the figure, the system calculates that the project is 1.67 percent complete. It's assuming that the hours budget has not changed from the original estimate, and so it has subtracted logged hours from bid hours to provide an "estimated hours to complete" number of 14,750. Now the project manager's real work begins: it's time to reforecast the hours.

To do so properly, the project manager must go through each of the five labor categories and estimate what he really thinks it will take to complete the tasks. He begins with engineering (which in this case means mechanical engineering), with 150 hours logged. Simple math against the budget says he'll need 2,850 more hours to complete this set of tasks. But is that really accurate? How can he possibly know? A sufficiently detailed analysis would be akin to painting the Eiffel Tower: as soon as he was finished with one, it would be time to start over.

The number of assumptions and guesses involved would likely make the whole effort of questionable value anyway.

This quandary leads many project managers to a simple but unsatisfactory solution: they stick with the original budgeted hours until they are far enough along in the project that hours forecasts become more manageable. Trouble is, that might be when they're 70 or 80 percent complete. No one can manage that much of a big project based purely on assumptions and guesswork.

Even Setpoint took that approach at first on the roller-coaster project, so in the first few weeks of the project, earned gross profit and forecast hours exactly matched the budget. The Joes knew that this was a red flag: on smaller projects, the numbers never matched exactly. Seeing an exact match on such a large project left them chilled to the bone: it meant they didn't really know what was going on. Obviously, they needed a better way of assessing their percent complete. Otherwise, it was just a matter of time before a big reforecasting miscalculation showed up to haunt them.

That was when they realized they could adapt an earned value table and incorporate it into their system.

Earned Value

Earned value tables are a primary tool in the *earned value management* (EVM) philosophy of project management. Wikipedia's is as good a definition as any. EVM, it says, "is a technique for measuring project performance and progress in an objective manner. EVM has the ability to combine measurements of scope, schedule, and cost in a single integrated system. Earned Value Management is notable for its ability to provide accurate forecasts of project performance problems." Neither earned value tables nor other EVM techniques are new. What's new here is how we incorporate an earned value table into the Project Management for Profit system.

An earned value table is simply a detailed list of all project tasks and subtasks, with each one assigned a percentage of the overall project and sometimes even a specific dollar value. In theory, the value of each task is recognized as earned when the task is completed. The amount of labor expended to complete the task doesn't enter the equation.

Setpoint, however, decided that, instead of using dollar values, it would assign each task and subtask a portion of the hours budgeted for the project. The hours would then be translated into a percentage of overall project hours. The project manager would calculate the percent complete of each subtask, and then that percentage of the task's hours would be claimed as earned, *regardless of how many hours had actually been applied to the project to complete that task.*

The crucial percent-complete number for the overall project would be automatically calculated by the earned value table once the project manager had put in the percent-complete figures for each task. The system would then produce a gross profit dollar value and GP/H to be claimed as earned for the week.

A Sample Table

Now let's go back to our coaster project example and see what a Setpoint earned value table would look like for the mechanical engineering task. As we saw, the project manager estimated that the mechanical engineering task would require 3,000 hours to complete.

Continuing to keep the example simple, we have broken down the mechanical engineering task into ten subtasks, each with an estimated value of 300 hours (see figure 8-3). In the real world, you would likely have many more subtasks, with a target value for each subtask of about 100 hours or less so you can get an accurate estimate.

FIGURE 8-3

Task name	Hours	% ach entry	Earned hours	Task % value	Earned % total
Project #6307 Super Coaster	15,000.00	0.00%	**0.00**		0.00%
			% subtask complete		
Mechanical engineering	3,000.00	0.00%	0.00	20.00%	
Concept	300.00		0.00	2.00%	
Customer specification analysis	300.00		0.00	2.00%	
Site plan analysis	300.00		0.00	2.00%	
Ride overall layout	300.00		0.00	2.00%	
Station layout	300.00		0.00	2.00%	
Lift layout	300.00		0.00	2.00%	
Structural component identification	300.00		0.00	2.00%	
Load calculations	300.00		0.00	2.00%	
FEA analysis	300.00		0.00	2.00%	
Overall system final review	300.00		0.00	2.00%	

Our ten subtasks are now entered beneath the primary task in the earned value table template. The table also lists the percentage value of the task and subtasks as they relate to the overall project. You can see in the example that the primary mechanical engineering task is 20 percent of the overall project value, and each subtask equates to 2 percent of the total. Once the project manager enters his estimates for each subtask, the template will roll up all of the completion percentages into a calculation of the number of hours earned, as well as an overall completion percentage for the entire project.

Granted, the project manager now must evaluate and report the status of ten small tasks, as opposed to the single, giant 3,000-hour task. While the job may seem more daunting than before—there are more tasks to analyze—in fact it is much more manageable, because each subtask is smaller.

So let's assume that the project manager has analyzed the subtasks and determined a current completion percentage for each one. He enters those numbers in the "percent achieved" field on the template (see figure 8-4). As you can see in the figure, the mechanical engineering team has earned 300 hours based on the cumulative completed percentages of the team's subtasks. If you recall the hours report from our example, we had only logged 150 actual hours on mechanical engineering to this point, so our team has been very efficient in its efforts: it has completed twice as much work as expected. The earned value table recognizes that fact and announces it to the world.

Once the project manager updates all of the subtasks for the whole project, the earned value table calculates the project's earned hours and overall percent complete. Though the hours report shows only 250 hours actually logged on

FIGURE 8-4

Task name	Hours	% ach entry	Earned hours	Task % value	Earned % total
Project #6307 Super Coaster	15,000.00		390.00		**2.60%**
			% subtask complete		
Mechanical engineering	3,000	10.00%	300.00	20.00%	
Concept	300	50.00%	150.00	2.00%	
Customer specification analysis	300	25.00%	75.00	2.00%	
Site plan analysis	300	10.00%	30.00	2.00%	
Ride overall layout	300	10.00%	30.00	2.00%	
Station layout	300	5.00%	15.00	2.00%	
Lift layout	300		0.00	2.00%	
Structural component identification	300		0.00	2.00%	
Load calculations	300		0.00	2.00%	
FEA analysis	300		0.00	2.00%	
Overall system final review	300		0.00	2.00%	

(continued)

FIGURE 8-4 *(continued)*

Task name	Hours	% ach entry	Earned hours	Task % value	Earned % total
Mechanical design	3,000.00	2.50%	% subtask complete	20.00%	
Task #1	300.00	25.00%	75.00	2.00%	
Task #2	300.00		0.00	2.00%	
Task #3	300.00		0.00	2.00%	
Task #4	300.00		0.00	2.00%	
Task #5	300.00		0.00	2.00%	
Task #6	300.00		0.00	2.00%	
Task #7	300.00		0.00	2.00%	
Task #8	300.00		0.00	2.00%	
Task #9	300.00		0.00	2.00%	
Task #10	300.00		0.00	2.00%	
Mechanical assembly	3,000.00	0.50%	% subtask complete	20.00%	
Task #1	300.00	5.00%	15.00	2.00%	
Task #2	300.00		0.00	2.00%	
Task #3	300.00		0.00	2.00%	
Task #4	300.00		0.00	2.00%	

			% subtask complete	
Task #5	300.00		0.00	2.00%
Task #6	300.00		0.00	2.00%
Task #7	300.00		0.00	2.00%
Task #8	300.00		0.00	2.00%
Task #9	300.00		0.00	2.00%
Task #10	300.00		0.00	2.00%
Electrical assembly	3,000.00	0.00%	0.00	20.00%
Task #1	300.00		0.00	2.00%
Task #2	300.00		0.00	2.00%
Task #3	300.00		0.00	2.00%
Task #4	300.00		0.00	2.00%
Task #5	300.00		0.00	2.00%
Task #6	300.00		0.00	2.00%
Task #7	300.00		0.00	2.00%
Task #8	300.00		0.00	2.00%
Task #9	300.00		0.00	2.00%
Task #10	300.00		0.00	2.00%

(continued)

FIGURE 8-4 (*continued*)

Task name	Hours	% ach entry	Earned hours	Task % value	Earned % total
			% subtask complete		
Installation	3,000.00	0.00%	0.00	20.00%	
Task #1	300.00		0.00	2.00%	
Task #2	300.00		0.00	2.00%	
Task #3	300.00		0.00	2.00%	
Task #4	300.00		0.00	2.00%	
Task #5	300.00		0.00	2.00%	
Task #6	300.00		0.00	2.00%	
Task #7	300.00		0.00	2.00%	
Task #8	300.00		0.00	2.00%	
Task #9	300.00		0.00	2.00%	
Task #10	300.00		0.00	2.00%	

the project, the earned value table is indicating 390 earned hours. The calculated completion percentage for the overall project now sits at 2.6 percent, as opposed to the 1.67 percent that the hours report had calculated. On a project of this size, that differential can easily translate to tens of thousands of dollars.

Evidently, the project team has been resourceful and industrious. Perhaps team members felt they were making exceptional progress in that first week. Now they can actually quantify it.

Thanks to the earned value table, the project manager in our example now has a completion percentage that he can confidently use to calculate the earned gross profit for the week. As a bonus, he can make sure the whole company knows how well his team did in the first week of the project. Conventional project management tools can't provide that information.

Breaking Down the Tasks

When you begin preparing earned value tables, you're likely to find that you need help from your project team in breaking each blob down into subtasks. One of the key questions you'll confront, for instance, is how small the subtasks should be to allow for effective management. The goal should be a level of disaggregation that considers all of the following criteria:

- The subtasks must be small enough to be easily monitored and analyzed. It helps to establish a standard maximum size for subtasks to use as a guideline. In most cases, the more you can break down a list of tasks, the better your chances of accurately tracking and measuring their levels of completion.

- All required tasks must be represented on the list, regardless of size or perceived importance. Very small tasks may be rolled in with other subtasks, but any task that requires labor hours should appear on the table.

- Vagueness or gray areas within the task list should be eliminated as much as possible. Kill the blobs. You are trying to minimize the amount of subjective input required and thereby get a clear view of the project's status.

In our business, keeping subtasks at 100 hours or less is a good starting point for developing an earned value table. Team leaders can easily manage subtasks of this size, and the work required to track tasks at that level is minimal.

The earned value table has a couple of side benefits as well.

For one thing, it mitigates the risk of inaccuracy by breaking down the tasks. It's like hedging a bet. If you have properly segregated the tasks on your table, you have lessened the chances of inaccurate reporting. If you do record an inaccurate figure on a small subtask, it affects overall project completion status to only a small degree.

It also creates tangible touchstones for the project team to use in monitoring and celebrating short-term goals for the project. In effect, it builds in the milestones that you need in any large project.

Now there's one more detail to resolve: the listed tasks and subtasks each must get an assigned value. This is where our twist on earned value table methodology comes most into play.

How Much Is That Subtask Worth?

Determining the value of each subtask can be the most daunting part of constructing an earned value table. There is always a certain amount of estimation and interpretation involved.

Since the amount of overall project gross profit in the Project Management for Profit system tends to fluctuate with the effects of COGS changes, we decided to calculate and recognize values for the table as percentages based on hours rather than revenue dollars or cost dollars. This way, as gross profit fluctuations came and went, the percentages would continually reflect an accurate picture of the work completed in the project.

And since project hours were already a key part of the system, we decided to use hours for designated values on the earned value table. As you saw in the roller-coaster example, if a project subtask has 300 hours in the budget and the project manager determines it's 50 percent complete, that task has earned 150 hours. If the team needed only 100 hours of actual labor to get to 50 percent, congratulations are in order. If it needed 250 hours, corrective action may be required.

To be sure, you can use other methods to assign values within an earned value table. Some systems use a weighted scale that assigns a higher value to tasks deemed to be of higher risk. Others have sliding valuation scales that record a higher value for early completion, and then a declining scale of value as a task gets more and more beyond its scheduled completion date. You should use whatever method of valuation works best for your business, but there are a few points you will want to consider when designing your system:

- It's best if you have a tangible correlation of some
  kind as a base for your valuations—that is, a relationship between the metric you're using and the actual degree of completion. The hours correlation works well for us, but other metrics can be used as well. One road construction company uses the tonnage of gravel deployed. The company knows exactly how much

gravel it needs for any given section, so gravel tonnage used compared to total tonnage works well as a metric for percent complete.

- Your valuation system should minimize arbitrary value assignments as much as possible. This is sometimes unavoidable on small subtasks, but a good correlation metric should help you determine the value of most larger tasks in a systematic manner.

- Once your task valuation exercise is complete, leave the values alone. It's tempting to constantly adjust the valuations based on new information or developments throughout the life of the project, but this practice creates more trouble than it's worth. Constant adjustment of valuations means more subjective interpretation and the likelihood of more errors. It can introduce oscillations into the system that cloud what is really happening. And really, there is little to be gained. Unless your initial valuation estimates are dramatically wrong, leave them alone and chalk it up to lessons learned for the next earned value table that you build.

In our experience, you will be pleasantly surprised at how efficient the process can be. The amount of effort required for the project manager to set up and maintain this kind of earned value table is about the same as the hours-reforecasting method. The initial list development occurs naturally as a byproduct of developing the schedule for the project.

And now we have come to the end of part II. This section of the book has presented the Project Management for Profit system in a nutshell: tracking materials (COGS), measuring percent complete through labor hours, calculating and tracking gross profit per hour, and using an earned value table when required. If you fell asleep reading these five chapters, read them again. Otherwise, you will not understand the Project Management for Profit system.

In part III, we'll show you how to use this system to get the most bang for your buck.

CHAPTER 8 TAKEAWAYS

- On big projects, you'll need to break tasks into bite-size chunks so you can accurately estimate percent complete. We recommend that no subtask should be longer than 100 hours.

- Make sure you are comfortable constructing an earned value table (see the "Earned Value" section of this chapter for a review).

PART THREE

GETTING THE MOST BANG FOR YOUR BUCK

CHAPTER 9

CREATING A SCOREBOARD

People have some peculiar traits. They aren't always content just to do as they're told. They like to know the reasons for doing A rather than B. They want to know how the whole job is progressing, and whether they themselves are doing good work. They want to *know the score*, just as they would if they were at a sports contest. Imagine watching a high-level basketball game with no scoreboard—you'd have to devote your full attention to keeping score rather than just enjoying the game.

The Project Management for Profit system is all about keeping score. So far, we've shown how the project manager can assess COGS costs and percent complete as accurately as possible, and how she can monitor gross profit and gross profit per hour on a weekly basis. Those are great indicators of how she's doing in bringing the project through to a successful completion, on time and on budget. But projects are a team sport. Every project manager depends on her team members, just as every coach depends on the players. Shouldn't they know the score, too?

We believe they should, which is why our system always incorporates some kind of *public scoreboard*. We have learned over the years that sharing the key indicators makes for far better project management in all sorts of ways. This chapter and the following one will describe how to set up a good scoreboard, and how to use it to manage your projects far more effectively than you could by yourself.

One note before we begin: we'll often assume in these chapters that you are comfortable sharing dollar figures with your project teams. That's how Setpoint and a lot of other high-performing project-based companies operate. It's a philosophy called open-book management, and it operates on two well-tested assumptions. One is that most people are capable of learning the basics of finance and can understand the numbers. The other is that seeing the financial information helps them make better decisions. Our experience supports both of these beliefs, and we definitely recommend giving open book a try.

However, we know from experience that many companies are not comfortable sharing financial data with anyone other than a few senior managers. And they aren't about to start sharing the numbers more broadly just because someone writes a book about a new system of project management. If that's the case with your company, don't despair—we'll show you at the end of this chapter how to get many of the benefits of the system without full disclosure of actual dollar amounts.

So let's examine how you can introduce your team to the knowledge you have gained so far—and how you can realize the payoffs of team-focused project management.

The Huddle

In their book *The Great Game of Business,* Jack Stack and Bo Burlingham describe the use of a weekly or biweekly all-hands gathering that they call the *huddle.* It's a regular meeting to review the past week's or past month's performance and to look ahead to the coming period. (If you're not familiar with American football, the huddle is the brief get-together before every play, where the quarterback tells the others what the next play will be.) This kind of information sharing came to be a key part of the Project Management for Profit system.

A regular huddle lets project managers update their teams on all the important information, including:

- Individual project status reports.

- Project financial updates, such as "How much gross profit did we make last week on each project?" or "What's our running total on each project?"

- Cumulative finances for the company, both for the previous week and for the month. This is the real score—whether the company is making money or not.

- Specific project-related issues, both good and bad.

- Anticipated issues and goals for the coming week.

The more information you share, the better prepared your team will be to act or react in the best interests of the project, and of course the company.

A good time to conduct the huddle is on Monday afternoon, after project managers have had time to gather and calculate all of the numbers for the preceding week. This schedule also gives the accountants time to take the project numbers and roll them up into the company's cumulative scores. A huddle should have a collaborative, interactive tone, with everyone encouraged to participate. It doesn't have to take long. Typically, each project manager spends a few minutes going through the key metrics and issues relating to his or her current projects. People ask questions and offer ideas about problems and solutions.

It's essential to establish a regular schedule. When the huddle happens every week, team members develop a sense of urgency. They know there will be an accounting of progress and profitability on their project every Monday, so they have a big incentive to meet their goals every day. If by chance one team member isn't working as hard as the rest, the other members will be able to identify the problem quickly and take corrective actions. If an individual just isn't capable of performing at the necessary level, he or she will usually move on to a job that doesn't involve such close scrutiny. The Project Management for Profit system is based on a high degree of accountability, which in turn requires (and encourages!) a sustained high level of performance.

The huddle poses a question, however: what is the best way to communicate all the information that the team needs to know every week? In our experience, simply handing out pieces of paper rarely has the necessary impact.

Scoreboards

At Setpoint, the solution to the information-sharing problem was simple.

By design, Setpoint was an engineering company. Its mentality and culture were pure engineer. And most engineers' first tool for brainstorming and problem solving is a simple whiteboard. Early ideas and concepts for solutions are almost invariably sketched out with a dry marker on a whiteboard before they ever see a CAD terminal. Setpoint was (and is today) a maze of whiteboards in every area of the business, including engineering, management, accounting, and the shop.

Reid Leland, one of Setpoint's project managers at the time, brought the scoreboard situation to a head one day by asking a simple question: "Why don't we just put a big whiteboard in the shop for the huddle numbers to be displayed on? We use whiteboards for everything else around here." At that point the company moved its huddle information from a printed spreadsheet to large whiteboards with the numbers displayed for all to see. At this writing, Setpoint has been sharing its information in this manner for fifteen years.

Of course, it takes more time to put all the numbers on a whiteboard. You have to do it by hand. You have to be sure you get the numbers in the right places and that all the digits are accurate. But the size and impact of the numbers really highlight how each project is performing. Everyone sees the data, and not just in the huddle but all the time. People learn to watch the numbers the way they track any indicator of their performance. Visitors to Setpoint often see a shop technician standing to one side of the board as someone puts up the numbers. Armed with a calculator, the tech is trying to get a head start on the week.

Whiteboards might not work for every company. Technology companies, where everyone carries a laptop, might find it better to use computer-based spreadsheets or some kind of document-sharing software. And of course that approach is essential whenever a project team is geographically dispersed. Even so, we urge you to find ways to bring color and other design elements into the mix. Make it as big as you can. Not many things are as boring as a page filled with small, dull, gray numbers. And little is as fascinating as a scoreboard page where the most important numbers leap right out at you—particularly if you know exactly what each one means to you and your team.

Team Scoreboards

As you map out your scoreboard format, you'll find that you already have most of the basic categories. The GP/H worksheet contains all of the individual project data that you'll want to convey to your team, so a big portion of the scoreboard looks just like a large, wall-mounted GP/H worksheet (see figure 9-1).

FIGURE 9-1

Team Alpha Projects

Proj #	Current % comp	Prev % comp	Project revenue	Bid COGS	Actual COGS	Project GP	Earned GP	Previous GP	Week GP	Week hours	Week GP/HR	To date	Bid GP/HR
2221.00	90.00%	85.00%	$1,000,000	$500,000	$450,000	$550,000	$495,000	$490,000	$5,000	50.00	$100.00	$130.26	$125.00
2222.00	25.00%	20.00%	$2,000,000	$1,000,000	$1,100,000	$900,000	$225,000	$200,000	$25,000	150.00	$166.67	$112.50	$153.85
2223.00	2.00%	0.00%	$5,000,000	$2,500,000	$2,500,000	$2,500,000	$50,000	$0	$50,000	350.00	$142.86	$142.86	$125.00
									$80,000	**550.00**	**$145.45**	Totals	

Team Alpha Weekly Totals

GP	Hours	GP per hour
$80,000	550.00	$145.45

Each project has its own line on the scoreboard, and all of the data from the project manager's GP/H worksheets translates directly to the board. This includes running gross profit totals, updated COGS information, hours invested to date, and weekly and cumulative project GP/H. In essence, the team looks directly at a whiteboard version of the worksheet while members discuss their projects. All the data is laid bare for all to see, digest, and dissect.

Company Scoreboard

But the team scoreboard covers only part of the information you may want to share. You can also display your company's cumulative gross profit and expenses. This requires a larger whiteboard, something like what is shown in figure 9-2.

The cumulative board lists details on each of the following financial metrics:

- Individual team cumulative scores for the week.

- Weekly and monthly earned gross profit for the entire company.

- Weekly earned gross profit totals.

- Weekly and monthly operating expenses (OE).

- Direct and overhead hours for the week and the month, as well as the critical percent-direct number.

- Weekly and monthly GP/H.

- GP-OE, or what accountants call operating profit or EBIT.

- Finally, the key number: GP/OE. By tracking this one metric, anyone can tell how well or poorly the company has been doing from a financial perspective.

FIGURE 9-2

Setpoint Cumulative Board					
	GP forecast	**GP actual**	**Delta**	**Hours**	**GP/HR**
Team Alpha	$70,000	$80,000	$10,000	550.00	$145.45
Team Beta	$65,000	$88,000	$23,000	650.00	$135.38
Totals	$135,000	$168,000	$33,000	1,200.00	$140.00

Week 3 totals	
Total GP	$168,000
Weekly OE	$85,000
Weekly GP-OE	$83,000
Weekly GP/OE	1.98

Monthly forecast numbers	
GP	$540,000
OE	$300,000
GP/OE	1.80
GP-OE	$240,000

Month cumulative	Week 1	Week 2	Week 3	Week 4	Running totals
Actual weekly GP	$140,000	$130,000	$168,000		$438,000
Forecast weekly GP	$135,000	$135,000	$135,000	$135,000	$540,000
Delta	$5,000	($5,000)	$33,000		($102,000)
Weekly cost	$70,000	$75,000	$85,000		$230,000
Direct hours	1,000	1,050	1,200		3,250
Overhead hours	300	300	300		900
% direct	70%	71%	75%		72%
GP per hour	$140.00	$123.81	$140.00		$134.77
Cost per hour	$70.00	$71.43	$70.83		$70.75
Running total GP/OE	2.00	1.73	1.98		1.90

In the huddle, project managers go through their project updates and answer any questions that crop up. Then a member of the management team walks people through the main numbers from the company scoreboard. While all of the numbers are open for discussion, you will definitely want to discuss the following every week, assessing both the absolute numbers and the trend lines:

- Total earned gross profit versus the gross profit forecast for the week and cumulative for the month

- OE cost per hour for the week and cumulative for the month

- GP/OE for the week and cumulative for the month

- Percent direct for the week and cumulative for the month

- GP/H for the week and cumulative for the month

With just a few minutes of discussion and explanation, it will be clear to everyone how the company is doing financially *right now*. Encourage questions and try to answer them thoroughly to ensure that everyone has the same understanding of each metric presented in the huddle.

The Scoreboards' Effects

A big part of the huddle's—and the scoreboard's—effectiveness lies in how they influence people's motivations and behavior. In particular, they encourage both the project manager and the team to address any issues or ideas for innovation that are likely to affect the project's profitability. The problems are right there on the scoreboard, every Monday. No one can hide from them, and they never go away on their own. That by itself gives people a reason to deal with issues quickly.

Incidentally, we're not referring only to practical issues of project execution. The scoreboards have a way of bringing complex interpersonal issues to the fore as well.

Several years ago, for example, Setpoint had landed a project with about $200,000 of revenue and $90,000 budgeted for COGS. It called for 850 hours of labor. Work out the math and you can see that budgeted GP/H was a stellar $129.41. Everyone could see that this project would really help the company's bottom line and improve the prospects for bonuses.

The first week, the project manager posted the numbers on the board, showing COGS right on budget and 50 hours spent. But his percent complete was only 4.2, rather than the 5.9 that the technicians—quick with their calculators—expected. "Why the difference?" someone asked. The manager explained: he had decided the project would require 1,200 hours rather than the budgeted 850. "The salespeople always underestimate what it really takes to get a job done," he declared. "Instead of getting blamed for getting behind later, I just added how much I thought the job was underestimated and added it at the beginning."

Wow. That decision meant that budgeted GP/H was only $91.67 rather than $129.41. The difference would come right out of the company's profit and hurt the chances of a bonus. The whole team was concerned about the issue—but, interestingly, not everyone agreed. Salespeople were upset by the assumption that they didn't know their job. Some of the technicians voiced the opinion that maybe this project manager had a point—those guys in sales always come up with tight budgets that we have to fight to meet. A sales rep retorted that if they padded budgets the way the techs seemed to want, the company would never win any work.

In effect, the huddle and scoreboard had revealed a serious problem that was hurting both profit and morale. At Setpoint, it came to be known as TWIT, an acronym for "takes whatever [time] it takes." When project teams felt the budget was too aggressive, they would disregard the budgeted plan and add hours. Left unchecked, this kind of problem can kill a company.

Setpoint solved the problem by instituting an internal bid review process in which salespeople, engineers, and project managers all discussed and reviewed bids before submission.

Today, everyone's in agreement about the budget before the project bid even goes out the door. You may want to do something similar in your company.

A "Scoreboard Culture"

Companies that succeed with the Project Management for Profit system build it into their culture. It's not a sideshow that is somehow tacked on to the business, nor is it simply a new accounting method. Rather, it is a central set of principles that guide the conduct of the enterprise. Part of this culture is a rigorous accountability—which, as we noted, is not right for every employee. Some people just don't want to know the financial numbers of their business, and they don't want that degree of accountability. However, people who feel empowered by facts and numbers will tend to stick around longer. These people value the truth, and their ability to act on the truth makes them valuable team members.

Such a culture doesn't materialize out of thin air. You may want to begin short, regular classes to teach the fundamentals of the system and the underlying philosophies. The classes can cover the various metrics and the use of the scoreboards. The most effective ones last no longer than twenty or thirty minutes, so you'll want to divide the information into small chunks. Remember to gear the classes to people at every level of financial understanding, and to reward attendees for their engagement. Some companies let team members earn T-shirts and coffee mugs for attending classes; others provide a free pizza lunch. Whatever the specifics, a little education goes a long way toward helping people to understand the system and to make it a regular part of daily life in the business.

A bonus plan for all employees that is tied directly to the company's overall profitability will also help maintain interest by giving people some skin in the game. While a bonus plan isn't necessary for the system to work effectively, it does get people's attention. At Setpoint, for example, everyone knows that wins and losses on projects directly affect their bonus checks. The status of the bonus appears on the weekly boards, since all the critical data for calculating the bonus pool is there already.

Other techniques can help sustain employees' interest and develop their skills. For example, try giving everyone a short financial quiz after a brief discussion on the postclose financials for the preceding month. Ask about everything from GP/H to operating expense levels. Perhaps team members can earn bonus points for completing and turning in the financial quizzes every month—points that increase their share of the bonuspool money. Before long, you're likely to find that people are pretty sharp when it comes to business finances.

There are plenty of other ways to reinforce the core philosophies of the system. Whatever method you use, remember this: if you let up, even a little, from your conviction to imbed the new system and its philosophies in your company's culture, it can wither on the vine. People sense that kind of hesitation and may rebel against the change. By contrast, once they see that you and the company are committed—that the system is going to happen with or without them—even the stubborn ones will likely embrace the change. Eventually, people will act and react as they are expected to because "that's the way we do things around here."

When You Can't Share Financial Information

Much of this chapter assumes that you are prepared to share financial data with employees, as open-book companies do. That works for many companies, but not for all.

Sometimes sharing actual dollar figures runs counter to the wishes of the company's owners or senior executives. If your company is publicly traded, you may encounter concerns about running afoul of Securities and Exchange Commission rules. If that's the case, you can still use the Project Management for Profit system and take advantage of its benefits. It's the process and the discipline it fosters that make it work, not the dollar figures themselves.

A common substitute for dollars, for instance, is to use an *efficiency percentage* to monitor the project's progress. In this method, we'll assume that the project manager knows the dollar figures but can't share them. Instead, he calculates the dollar-per-hour figures from the original project budget numbers and then translates that into a percentage number for the team.

Here's an example that shows how it works:

- The project's budget calculations tell the project manager that the expected GP/H rate for the job is $100.

- The project manager sets the $100-per-hour mark as "100 percent efficiency" for the project.

- After completing his weekly financial calculations, he finds that the team has earned $120 in gross profit for every hour invested during the previous week. In other words, his team has performed at 120 percent efficiency for the week.

- He shares that figure with the team and offers congratulations to all. The team now has a clear metric that quantifies their efforts and provides a hard goal for efficiency throughout the project.

You can use something similar for internal projects with predetermined time budgets. Your metric can measure efficiency by comparing hours worked to hours earned based on the hours budget or on an earned value table. As long as you have some metric that reflects progress (and issues) on the project accurately, the system will work as well as it does with dollars.

CHAPTER 9 TAKEAWAYS

- You can't get the benefits of team help unless you share the data every week. Team members must understand what the numbers mean if they are to help solve the inevitable problems. If your company's culture needs to change to allow this kind of sharing, be the change agent yourself.

- A visual scoreboard is best if you can create one.

- Bad news doesn't get better with time. A weekly scoreboard and huddle force everyone to deal with reality.

CHAPTER 10

REALIZING ALL THE BENEFITS

The primary benefit of the Project Management for Profit system lies in the magic word we mentioned in the previous chapter: *accountability*. The weekly huddle creates high levels of accountability for every person who touches the project. The project manager, of course, is most in the spotlight, for better or worse. But everyone on the team feels the same pressures. This stress-balancing, as it might be called, fosters a number of positive behaviors. Hallway conversations begin to focus on what the boards will show on the coming Monday. Team members tune in to the ups and downs of the project and tend to work more closely together than project teams we've seen at other companies. Knowledge is power—and the more knowledge the team has, the better its daily decisions.

A company that operates this way is also likely to see some spillovers from the high level of accountability. Separate project teams may begin to compete with each other, because their performance has been converted into a common financial score. In the example shown in figure 10-1, you can see that while

FIGURE 10-1

Setpoint Cumulative Board					
	GP forecast	**GP actual**	**Delta**	**Hours**	**GP/HR**
Team Alpha	$70,000	$80,000	$10,000	550.00	$145.45
Team Beta	$65,000	$88,000	$23,000	650.00	$135.38
Totals	$135,000	$168,000	$33,000	1,200.00	$140.00

Week 3 totals	
Total GP	$168,000
Weekly OE	$85,000
Weekly GP-OE	$83,000
Weekly GP/OE	1.98

Monthly forecast numbers	
GP	$540,000
OE	$300,000
GP/OE	1.80
GP-OE	$240,000

Month cumulative	Week 1	Week 2	Week 3	Week 4	Running totals
Actual weekly GP	$140,000	$130,000	$168,000		$438,000
Forecast weekly GP	$135,000	$135,000	$135,000	$135,000	$540,000
Delta	$5,000	($5,000)	$33,000		($102,000)
Weekly cost	$70,000	$75,000	$85,000		$230,000
Direct hours	1,000	1,050	1,200		3,250
Overhead hours	300	300	300		900
% direct	70%	71%	75%		72%
GP per hour	$140.00	$123.81	$140.00		$134.77
Cost per hour	$70.00	$71.43	$70.83		$70.75
Running total GP/OE	2.00	1.73	1.98		1.90

both teams had pretty good weeks, Alpha team's performance was just a little better than Beta team's. Alpha definitely held the bragging rights for the week—and Beta team members may try extra hard to win the title of Most Profitable Team for the following week.

A little competition of this sort is healthy. But there's an even more interesting behavior that often emerges as well. If one team is struggling to keep its project profitable and on time, other teams may raise their games to offset the potential negatives. The help might involve suggestions designed to improve the ailing project, or it might mean increasing the productivity of the successful teams' own projects to counter the losses from the laggard. Competitiveness rarely gets in the way of concern for the company's overall financial health, particularly when all of the project teams share the wins and losses in the form of a bonus.

In companies that don't use the Project Management for Profit system, the definition of success varies greatly from one group to another. Engineers consider a project successful if their solutions worked well. Marketing calls it successful if the customer is happy. Only the accountants and senior management actually measure the project's outcome based on financial results. At a company using our system, by contrast, everyone has the same goals for the project. The first goal is to make a profit; the second is to make the customer happy; and the third is to provide elegant, robust solutions. While the technical and marketing achievements of the project are important, they are secondary to the goal of profitability. The reason, of course, is that profitability determines a company's survival. Only by making that goal number one can a company continue playing the game.

Additional Benefits of the System

When you begin to change the way people think and act, as the Project Management for Profit system does, you are likely to find some unexpected benefits. We have observed several over the years, both at Setpoint and at other companies.

Tracking Cash Flow

One of the simplest and most easily realized benefits is the ease with which you can track your cash flow.

Nearly every project-based company bills its customers based on project milestones. Our system's weekly tracking of schedules and percent complete makes it easy to predict exactly when you can send out an invoice. So that lets you anticipate cash inflows. At the same time, you are watching material costs (COGS) and operating expenses weekly. Put those two together and it's easy to track cash outflows. The combination of inflows and outflows lets you predict net cash for the next few months, and spot potential cash crunches well in advance. Believe us: your bankers will love you for it.

Eliminating Sandbagging

The other benefits are in some ways more surprising. Consider the phenomenon of sandbagging. In project management, *sandbagging* refers to the practice of holding back positive results until the end of a project and then taking a big windfall when the project is complete. It's a common practice, and project managers often try to justify it. They are saving the gains for a rainy day. They are waiting to make sure the gain is real. Those are fine practices up to a point, but sandbaggers take it beyond that point and so produce poor assessments of a project's progress. While the sandbagging manager's intentions are usually good, the outcome is always a less-than-accurate picture of where the project and the company really stand.

The Project Management for Profit system puts severe constraints on sandbagging; indeed, it is likely to lead to quick self-correction. Here's an example from our experience:

> The project in question was moving along quite
> well. Good planning and execution, combined with
> some luck, had put the team right on the brink of

completing the project, on budget and ahead of schedule. But a look at the financial board during the weekly huddle showed that the project was only about 70 percent complete, with GP/H just about dead-on with the budgeted rate. The project manager said his piece during the huddle and then asked the group for questions. No one voiced any concerns, but several team members had befuddled looks on their faces. When the huddle was over, everyone went back to work.

Within an hour, two team members made separate visits to company managers, letting the managers know that they didn't believe the numbers presented for their project. They felt they had performed better than they were getting credit for. They had set and met goals, and they took pride in the gains that they thought they had made. But those gains weren't showing up on the board. One of the technicians said, "How can we be at 70 percent complete on this project when all we need to do is tighten a few bolts and shrink-wrap the machine for shipment?" He added that if the project were reported accurately, the team would share a great bonus that month.

One of the company's managers investigated the situation by going over the project's percent-complete calculations with the project manager. It soon became apparent that the project was indeed much farther along than the numbers that day had indicated. The project manager admitted that the project was ahead of schedule, but said he was nervous about some unknown issue coming into play that might negatively affect his results. Company managers persuaded him to revise his figures to reflect his real progress.

After a couple of self-corrections like this, the practice of sandbagging is likely to disappear. After all, you can't be speeding around town for long if every driver on the road has a radar gun and a ticket book. The board keeps the team and the project manager honest.

Tracking Change Orders

One of the most difficult tasks a project manager faces is serving as guardian of the project's scope. Making sure that the team delivers the agreed-upon features is hard enough. But if he doesn't succeed in policing scope creep, he will never bring his projects in on time and on budget.

If you're not familiar with the term *scope creep*, it works like this. Let's say you have contracted to develop a new mobile application for smart phones. The project clearly defined the features and specifications that this app would include. The customer is excited and has signed the contract. Before the project is finished, however, the customer decides he would like to add a couple of small features to increase the app's marketability. In fact, he has convinced one of the engineers—your employee— that this upgrade will really make a big difference. The engineer thinks the proposed features are cool, and he comes to see you to get your buy-in. It will hardly add any time, he promises, and the delivery date won't slip by more than a day or two. In fact he has already architected the change. All he needs now is a "go" signal from you.

This is a discussion that happens in every kind of project we're familiar with. In most cases, customers don't intend to chip away at your project's profitability. They merely want to get the best possible result, from their perspective. And, of course, customers sometimes can't visualize what the project will look like as it progresses. When they see it nearing completion, they suddenly get an inspiration about how to make it better. This is as common in home-bathroom remodeling jobs as it is in the complex machines that Setpoint builds for its customers. The bigger the customer's project team, the greater the risk of scope creep. You could call it Beach Boys syndrome: everybody begins singing, "Wouldn't it be nice . . .," just like the old Beach Boys song.

Faced with the inevitable requests for additional work, you must decide whether to take a hard line and require a change order, or else give in to the customer's pleas and do the extra work for nothing. In any one case, it might be easier just to add some features to the program or switch to a more expensive bathroom tile or do the additional digging. You can always write off the extra expense to customer relations. When you do that, however, you have thrown the door open for scope creep, and you will have to struggle to maintain your project's budget. For once the customer gets what he asks for, he's likely to ask for another change and then another.

The only sure way to inoculate your project against Beach Boys syndrome is to analyze and define every out-of-scope wish-list item and put a firm dollar figure on each one as you go along. Sometimes the process is cut-and-dried: you come up with an appropriate amount and increase the contract accordingly. But gray areas abound, and customers' budgets may not allow them to spend more on the project than they have committed to. So there's no way around it: you have to negotiate. Just do it right away. The worst thing you can do is save up all the change orders as the project goes along and present them to the customer at the end. If you do that, you are likely to face a serious backlash.

By the way, one thing we've seen over the years is how hard it is to make a profit from change orders. Usually, it's an accomplishment just to break even on them. Recovering the direct costs of a change order is seldom the problem. Typically, what gets you is hidden costs: loss of efficiencies due to project delays, expedited shipping charges to get the additional materials in as soon as possible, and overtime to get the project back on track after a change order derailment. The loss of momentum while the scope-creep items are sorted out is often a huge cost by itself, and one that few companies are able to measure accurately. We often track change orders as separate projects, rather than lumping the revenue and costs associated with each one in with the rest of the project. It helps us determine where the inevitable problems are coming from.

The Project Management for Profit system can't eliminate the challenges of scope creep. But it can mitigate them. The reason is that the system, the boards, and the huddle don't allow additional commitments of labor, materials, or both to hide in the accounting department until long after the job is over. All the data is right there for everyone to look at and question every day, and the project manager has to explain it weekly. Even if the project team is really efficient, the additional hours and costs associated with scope changes will make the project look bad on the board. Key metrics such as GP/H will start dropping, and the team will begin asking questions. As a result, the project manager is much less apt to let the customer have items on his wish list without charging for it.

We learned the benefits of the system some years ago in one of the most dramatic cases of scope creep that we had ever seen. Here's the Setpoint project manager's story:

> We had contracted to design and build two new
> automation machines for a local manufacturing plant.
> It was a fairly large contract for this customer, and we

were pleased to get the work. The machines would be used to assemble a product that had never been manufactured before. Though the product was new, the customer had a well-defined vision of the project scope and of how the machines had to function. So we bid the project close to the published scope of work. We won the bid, and now we had a given amount of money to complete the designs and build the machines.

Approximately two weeks into the design process, the customer notified us that his team had "slightly modified" the product design. He said he would send us a new drawing reflecting the changes. Looking at the drawing, we saw that most of our design work up to that point had to be discarded. We groaned at the prospect, but we forged ahead to get the project back on track. I immediately told our customer that accommodating his changes would involve additional costs. He said he realized there would be a change order involved. He also asked me to continue tracking the additional charges, because there would be probably be more. Little did we know, that was just the beginning.

Over the next six months, the customer presented us with many changes to the product design. Even during the construction phase, he tinkered with this or that detail, causing extra expenditures for labor and materials nearly every day. We tracked every penny. We had to so we could answer to our own team members and management in the weekly huddles. In fact, to keep the change order items straight, we tracked all the extra work separately, as its own project. The numbers were piling up, and we began to be concerned about how big the "change order project" would eventually become.

I sent regular updates to the customer so that he knew how much the tab was building up every week.

In the end, the total for all of the extra work was more than the original contract. While the customer's management team wasn't pleased, nobody disputed the amount since we had shared regular weekly running totals, along with details of all of the work and materials required by the changes. They got their machines, and we got paid for all the inefficiencies and extra work caused by their changes.

If your project-tracking system lets nothing slip under the radar, either you get paid for the extra work, or the customer declines to pay and the work isn't done. There are really no other options when all the facts are out in the open.

Providing Weekly Customer Updates

Regular, accurate communication with your customers can help you through just about any situation. Even when things are going poorly, the more you inform the customer about the status of things, the better it is for everyone. An essential part of the Project Management for Profit system is weekly customer updates. Every project manager should send out an update to every customer once a week. Figure 10-2 shows what such an update might look like. It lists the project's percent complete, the expected delivery date, and a few key points about the project's current status.

In the example shown, you can see that the project is listed as 11.65 percent complete. This is the same figure that the project manager uses to calculate the project's earned GP. (You can see how easily sandbagging could freak out a customer: "What do you mean it's only 70 percent complete? It's supposed to deliver Monday!")

FIGURE 10-2

Weekly Project Update

Project engineer: Dave Smith Project manager: Rob Johnson	Customer: American Manufacturing
Project no.: 2221	Customer contact: Bob Jones
Project description: Robotic load system	Customer fax/email: bob.jones@amfact.usa.com

Project scope status

Project 11.65% complete:
- System electrical and mechanical design are ongoing
- Design review is scheduled for Sept 14
- Robots are ordered and set for Oct 1 delivery

Project schedule status (see attached schedule)

	Baseline delivery date	Dec 17
Variances due to changes to project scope	Schedule impact	
Concept change impact in design time-frame	2 weeks	
Total approved variances		
	Adjusted baseline	Dec 31
Setpoint variances	Schedule impact	
Total Setpoint variances		
Customer variances	Schedule impact	
Total customer variances		
	Project delivery date	Dec 31

Project budget status

Date	PO#	Description	Status	Amount
May 17	5555555555	Robotic load system per spec Amfact 1.243-section 11 thru 17	A	$680,210.00
			Total	$680,210.00

The example also lists a two-week variance on the project delivery date due to a design change from the customer. The projected delivery date accounts for the two-week delay. These changes remain on the updates throughout the project's life and can be quickly referenced when the question comes up down the road, "What two-week delay?"

It's a good idea to tailor your update sheets to address points that are particularly relevant to certain customers. The updates might include photos, sketches, test results, calculations, and anything else that can help the customer understand exactly what's going on. You want to put together a tightly packaged executive summary that the customer can read and understand quickly. Your contact can then hand the same report to her own project team, quickly bringing everyone up to speed on the progress of the project and any hurdles that may have cropped up. This kind of information sharing helps create a better partnership between vendor and customer. Even if the going is tough, it always pays to have the customer know the status of things.

Too many project managers share only the good news; they keep the bad news under wraps and try to make up for it secretly. Maybe that works sometimes. When it doesn't, though, things can get ugly. An ambushed customer who had no idea there was a problem is now faced with the fact that, yes, there is indeed a big problem—and it's too late to do anything about it.

The following story illustrates this point. It's true, but we have changed the identities of the involved parties to save them from embarrassment. By the way, the company in the story is another of the many project-based companies that are now bankrupt.

The project was running about three months behind schedule. It had been a bunch of little things that had added up to the delay, so it didn't happen all at once. We had seen it coming for months. In every discussion regarding the project, we mentioned the delays. But Richard, our company's vice president, repeatedly stressed that the lost time had to be made up before the project deadline. He wasn't about to tell the customer that the project was going to be late.

As the delivery date drew close, the customer sent several representatives out to our factory to look at the equipment that was supposedly due to be shipped any day. What they found was a project that was still three months away from completion. There was ranting and yelling, threats of lawsuits, and general mayhem for the next three days.

After an intense conference call with the customer's president, Richard called a meeting of his staff and briefed them on the outcome. "OK," he said, "we seem to have calmed the customer down. They understand that they need to delay their grand opening. We've got to make up at least a month of our lost time, and we'll be all right. But we did learn one very important fact about this particular customer. It turns out that if we're slipping behind, they want to know about it early. That's good to know."

Good to know? Holy cow. This customer wasn't an equal partner in the game. Richard had chosen to exclude the customer from the bad news until there was nothing that could be done to mitigate the delay. The fact that the customer would have liked to know about the problem three months earlier was a revelation.

To turn from the negative to the positive, here's a story from Setpoint's recent past that highlights the value of a full-disclosure partnership with the customer:

> Setpoint was building a small roller coaster for a major amusement park. The coaster was just one piece of a major park upgrade. There were dozens of contractors involved and a very aggressive schedule, as is usually the case with amusement park projects.
>
> As Setpoint got deep into the project, several issues arose that negatively affected our coaster's schedule. We immediately notified the customer, and we adjusted delivery dates months ahead of time. By the end of the project, we had delivered the coaster about six weeks later than the original delivery date. We weren't happy about it, but the customer had been in the loop every step of the way.
>
> When the whole thing was complete, the park held an award ceremony to congratulate the contractors on the successful completion of the job. Setpoint got an award as the only contractor that delivered on time. Even though we were six weeks late, the customer didn't feel that we were late because he had been a part of the date adjustment process months before. And if your customer doesn't think you're late, then you're not.

No question, the more you can do to make your customer feel like an equal partner in the project, the better the results for everyone involved. Giving them all the news, good or bad, helps to develop and sustain a level of trust between the parties that makes it easier for everyone to get what they need out of the project.

CHAPTER 10 TAKEAWAYS

- The Project Management for Profit system will be most successful when there is accountability at all levels and for all the individuals associated with the project.

- Side benefits of the system include tracking cash flow, eliminating sandbagging, and understanding when change orders are appropriate.

- Weekly communication with the customer is essential. It should include all the critical elements of the project.

CHAPTER 11

WHAT IF THERE IS NO EXTERNAL CUSTOMER?

As you have probably noticed, most of the examples in this book come from project-based companies. Project-based companies build houses, dig ditches, create software, mount publicity campaigns, design machines, perform financial audits, manage conferences and other events, and perform countless other tasks. But they all have one thing in common. Each project has an outside customer who agrees to pay a certain amount for the work involved. The team's job is to deliver the project on time and on budget, and thus earn a profit for the company.

Plenty of projects, however, take place inside operating companies—companies whose business involves regular, repeated tasks rather than individual projects. Operating companies include manufacturers, distributors and retailers, service providers such as insurance companies, and so on. The projects that these companies sponsor, typically, are internal initiatives designed to further their business. A manufacturer might install a new automation line, launch a new marketing campaign, or develop a new product in its R&D lab. A retailer might open a store in another city or create a new e-commerce site. A service provider might put in a new telecommunications system or revamp its Web site. The possibilities are endless, but they, too, have one thing in common. There is no external customer. The customer is the company itself, which is making an investment in its future.

Internal projects, as we'll call them, resemble conventional external-customer projects in many ways. They typically have specified goals and a timeline ("Get the new telecom system up and running by December 1"). They generally have a project manager, although in this case he may have another job within the company as well.

Internal projects also have budgets. But here's where they often diverge from external-customer projects.

Let's say Northwest Supply builds a new store or buys and installs a new computer system. The company naturally creates a budget for everything it has to purchase from outside—materials and equipment, contractors' services, consultants, and so on. This budget is the equivalent of COGS in the Project Management for Profit system.

Northwest also expects to devote a certain amount of internal resources—management time, specialized labor, and the like—to the project. It may or may not write down how much of these resources it proposes to spend. If the project requires a large amount of internal resources, most companies do indeed create a budget for those resources. But many not-too-big projects have no internal budget. The executive in charge tells the project manager, "Feel free to draw on the IT department for programming support, so long as they get their regular work done," or "You can use our design shop for the marketing campaign—I'm sure Cheryl can free up somebody for a couple of weeks."

Just to be clear what we're talking about here, we should distinguish between projects that require budgets and tracking and those that don't. Every company has very small projects, and every company has what might be called side jobs. Very small projects and side jobs don't need any kind of management system. Whoever is responsible for them can assess progress just by looking and can keep the relevant numbers on a sheet of paper or in a simple Excel file. If you're responsible for updating the employee handbook or planning the company picnic, you won't need an elaborate system for tracking your progress or your budget. The topic of this chapter is not small projects or side jobs, it's good-sized projects with a budget ranging from $100,000 up into the millions and an internal time requirement of 200 hours or more.

If you're managing this kind of internal project, you can and should use the Project Management for Profit system. But for it to work, you will have to set your project up properly. This chapter describes how to do so.

Allocate Enough of Your Own Time—and Your Team's

The first requirement should go without saying, except that would-be project managers regularly get themselves into trouble by ignoring it. No one can manage a project of any size and complexity while simultaneously holding down a demanding day job. If your company wants you to run a good-sized project, make it plain that you will need to devote so many hours every week to the project, and that your other responsibilities will need to be adjusted accordingly. Otherwise, you are setting yourself up to fail.

The same goes for everyone else who will be putting a significant amount of time into the project. Once you figure out how many hours of each person's time you will need (see the following section), make sure that those people actually have that much time to give—and that their supervisors won't be expecting them to do 100 percent of their regular jobs while they are involved in the project.

Break the Project Down into Bite-Size Chunks

Every project involves a number of discrete tasks. People need to perform these tasks at the right time. Some must be performed sequentially, one after the other. Others can move in parallel. Veteran managers of specific kinds of projects know from experience what the tasks are, and they can easily create a chart showing what has to happen when. Novices should get help in doing this, because it's easy for a rookie to overlook some key steps.

A friend of ours, for example, a computer programmer, was building a house for his family, and he decided to act as his own general contractor. He hired an architect, got a set of plans, arranged for all the permits, and so on. He lined up an excavator to dig the basement, a concrete supplier to assemble the forms and pour the concrete, a plumber, an electrician, a wallboard company, and a painter. He planned to do much of the carpentry himself, with the help of a friend. He described the work plan in general terms to his uncle, who was a contractor in another state; the uncle said it sounded OK. Everything went remarkably smoothly, until near the end.

That was the day when the town's building inspector stopped by. As any contractor knows, the inspector has to do a four-way inspection, checking the electrical, plumbing, heating and air-conditioning, and insulation before the walls are closed in. Our friend had forgotten that fact, or maybe he never knew it. So the inspector found the walls all covered with Sheetrock, the joints taped and plastered. He immediately put a stop to the job and told our friend sorry, but those walls have to be opened up. The mistake wound up costing the amateur contractor many thousands of dollars. When he asked his uncle why he hadn't mentioned the inspection, the uncle replied, "I assumed you knew about that—everybody does." Then he added, "If you had given me a detailed work plan with individual tasks spelled out week by week, I'd have spotted what was missing in a minute."

Breaking the project down into bite-size chunks helps ensure that you don't make that kind of mistake. It also allows you to assign estimated labor time to each chunk and thus create a labor budget that is as accurate as possible. You can use the labor budget, in turn, to create an earned value table (see chapter 8) and to estimate percent complete as the project goes along. This is the only practical way of tracking your progress on a complex project, because many big steps may be taking place simultaneously.

Say, for example, you're a marketer with the credit-card division of a bank, and you are charged with overseeing a direct-mail marketing campaign going out to 10 million individuals. You first need to develop a plan outlining the scope of the campaign, the expected results, and the timeline, all within the confines of the budget you have negotiated with the responsible executive. Then you and your team need to acquire the best possible mailing lists; develop the content and design of the mailing piece and get it approved; check to be sure your business-reply facility with the postal service is active and funded; contract with printers for the mailing piece itself and the envelopes; and contract with a mailing house to assemble and mail the 10 million pieces. Meanwhile, you have to be sure your incoming-mail facility is geared up to handle the responses. Each of these tasks involves several subtasks, and it will help you enormously to list each one.

Create an Accurate Budget—and Track It

The budget has two components. One part is what our system calls the COGS budget, though you should remember that we have our own definition of COGS (see chapter 2 for a reminder if you need one). This should include *every* external expense—all the stuff you have to buy plus every outside contractor you will have to hire. To see how you are doing on COGS in this type of project, you simply need to compare your current COGS (actual and forecast) to the budget.

Note, however, that companies are often careless (sometimes deliberately so) in determining COGS budgets. Maybe they budget for the new telecom system but forget to include the cost of some necessary rewiring. Maybe they budget for a costly new piece of software but don't count the cost of training employees on the new system. We say that companies are sometimes deliberately careless because internal projects are often the pet projects of some ambitious executive, and he deliberately lowballs the cost to get the investment approved.

The second component is the internal budget—the management time and internal specialized labor you will require to bring the project to a successful completion. As project manager, you'll estimate the number of hours required from each employee to complete the tasks and all the subtasks you have outlined. You can then compare the hours spent on the project to the hours earned on the project's earned value table to get an accurate percent complete. For example, if you are 20 percent complete on a 500-hour project, you have earned 100 hours. If you actually spent 90 hours to get that far, you are ahead by 10 hours. If you have spent 120 hours, you know that you are behind and need to catch up.

If you want to convert those hours to dollars, you will need to work with someone in the finance department to put a dollar figure on every individual's hours. The dollar figure will build in not only the cost of the person's wages or salary but also all the prorated overhead expenses. Once you do that, you will have your internal project budget in dollars. With a complete budget in hand, you can track your project as you would any other using the Project Management for Profit system.

Here, too, a word of caution is in order. Some finance departments in operating companies are unaccustomed to tracking project expenses. Even those that are accustomed to projects may be surprised to learn that you want regular weekly reports of both COGS expenses and internal expenses. But these reports aren't hard to produce, and if you tell your friends in finance that the reports are essential to keeping the project on track and on budget, they are likely to be cooperative. On your end, of course, you will have to make sure that every project member tracks and records the time he or she spends on the project, so that you can provide finance with weekly summaries. Most employees of operating companies aren't used to careful time tracking, so they will need a little practice in generating accurate time sheets.

Run the Project as if it Were Your Own Business

Taking charge of a good-sized project is a big responsibility. Your company is entrusting you with a lot of money and (probably) the time of some of its key people. It's no different, really, from running a project in a project-based company. You don't have to earn a profit, of course, but it's your job to bring the project in on time and on budget. If you have overruns on either score, you're costing your company money and therefore profit.

So here's what we suggest: run the project just the way we describe in this book. Make it a *project*, not just a side job. Create benchmarks and milestones. Hold regular meetings and get your team involved. Put up a scoreboard so that everyone can track progress and can deal with issues or setbacks as a group. It's a business, and you are the CEO.

As we noted, if you have a full budget with dollar costs and COGS, you can use the complete Project Management for Profit system. Your revenue is the project budget. You watch COGS expenses just as we have outlined. You determine percent complete based on labor hours. You track GP/H just as if you had an external customer. The difference, of course, is that you don't have to make an actual profit. But the goal is the same: a higher GP/H. If GP/H is lower than budgeted, you know that you are running into potential cost overruns. If it is higher, you know you are saving your company money.

You can also measure your labor performance using an efficiency measure. Recall our earlier example, where you were 20 percent complete on a 500-hour project and had earned 100 hours. Earned hours divided by actual hours gives you a measure of efficiency. If you have actually spent 90 hours, your efficiency is $100 \div 90$, or 111 percent. If you have actually spent 120 hours, your metric is $100 \div 120$, or 83 percent. We sometimes use these efficiency metrics daily for some of our largest projects, just to make sure we are not getting off track.

Operating companies too often take a cavalier attitude toward their projects, and as a result the projects eat up time and money that could better be used elsewhere. If you use this system—better yet, if you teach it to your colleagues—you'll find that you are making a big difference in your unit's performance.

CHAPTER 11 TAKEAWAYS

- If an internal company project is big enough to have a budget, it's big enough to run using the techniques described in this book.

- Make sure you can control all the elements of the project. In particular, get time commitments from everyone who will participate. Make sure you can get all the data you need to manage the project, and be sure it is accurate.

- Track your project weekly with your team and follow the key metrics from chapter 6.

CHAPTER 12

THE THREE KEYS TO SUCCESS

This book describes a *system,* a set of tools and procedures for running projects that will help you keep your jobs on time and on budget. But notice that sneaky little word *help* in the preceding sentence. The Project Management for Profit system is a human system, not a mechanical one. It depends on what people—those imperfect, opinionated, stubborn biological entities—decide to say and do, day in and day out. If they choose, people can find a way to ignore or screw up any system. On the plus side, they can also figure out how to pitch in and make it work better.

In other words, nothing in this book will happen by itself. The success of the system depends on smart implementation. You will have to learn to introduce it, to run it smoothly, and to deal with the inevitable bumps along the road. You will have to build in the discipline required. We have had a great deal of experience with this at Setpoint, and we have seen many other companies implement the system with varying degrees of success. In this chapter, we'll offer three critical lessons on how to make it work.

First: Fly the Airplane

One of our friends is a military helicopter pilot who served a tour of duty in Afghanistan. He recently shared an unnerving experience with us.

We were called to support a group of marines in a convoy traveling to a village in southern Afghanistan. The marines were a special tactical group tasked to capture or eliminate a high-value target. We were in a team of two Apache helicopters, with a mission of providing air support.

The convoy began taking sporadic gunfire from a nearby hilltop. The marines asked my ship to eliminate the source of the gunfire. Arriving over the suspected enemy position, we found nothing but a sheep herder and his flock. He appeared to be minding his own business, but we knew that enemy combatants often disguised themselves as herders in this part of the country. We decided to continue our surveillance of him.

We circled the hilltop for about an hour and a half with this guy in our crosshairs, ready to fire the instant he showed any hostile intent. The only thing on our minds was successfully completing our task of suppressing the gunfire. Everything else became secondary. If we had been properly monitoring our instruments, we would have seen that a catastrophic failure was closing in on us.

Here's what we had hanging over our heads:

Prior to the call for support, we had started a fuel transfer to level the fuel tanks. This was normal, but in the heat of the moment we forgot to stop the transfer.

Soon one tank would be empty. Multiple gauges in the cockpit were warning me of this problem throughout the mission. I didn't notice them.

As time went on, moreover, the density altitude, or DA, increased significantly. As DA increases, power available decreases, and power required to maneuver the aircraft increases. The cockpit has multiple tools to help you assess and adjust for this condition, yet they also went unnoticed. We were totally focused on our target.

In this aircraft, draining one tank and filling the other leads to a single engine failure. A single engine failure at high altitude, with high DA and high power setting, reduces the speed of the rotor system and leads inevitably to a flaming hole in the ground.

When I finally brought my mind back inside the cockpit, I had emergency indications of zero fuel in the aft tank. I have no idea why the engine hadn't already failed, and I can only guess that I had mere seconds before it did. We broke off surveillance, got ourselves into a safer flight profile, and quickly corrected the fuel condition. When we returned to the hilltop, the enemy that we had been monitoring was gone.

Had we paid regular, disciplined attention to cross-checking all the gauges, metrics, and training that we had been provided with, the mission would have been safe and successful. Fortunately, we made it out alive and without any damage to our helicopter, but we let our intended target slip from our grasp.

One of the skills that military pilots practice regularly is continually cycling their attention between their target and their aircraft. The first priority is always the same in every situation: fly the airplane. Everything else is secondary, because if the airplane crashes, nothing else matters. Our friend had forgotten that axiom. He was suffering from what is known as *target fixation*, a laserlike focus on one objective to the exclusion of all else. He might easily have died from it.

People don't die from target fixation in business, but projects and companies crash and burn all the time because of it. People get focused on one goal—one target—to the exclusion of all else. Maybe they feel they absolutely have to bring the job in on time. Maybe they believe that they must wring every last cent of profit out of a project. They are suffering from target fixation, and it might be terminal. The reason is that no one objective and no one set of metrics ensures success.

That's true of the Project Management for Profit system as well. GP/H, for example, is critically important—it's a key to the whole thing. But other parts of the business are important as well. If you bring your project in on time and on budget but have somehow alienated the customer, you have effectively cut yourself off from future work for that customer. If you bring your project in on time and on budget but have ridden your employees so hard that half of them quit, you're unlikely to succeed in your next job. If your own GP/H is great but a key subcontractor falls down on the job, your project may fail anyway. Like a pilot, a project manager or company owner has to keep a weather eye on all the different gauges and indicators that determine long-term business success. Watch your objectives, yes—but above all, keep your plane in the air.

Second: Good Data Leads to Good Results

The Project Management for Profit system is built on data. It needs regular, accurate, timely information about COGS expenditures and labor hours above all. It also needs a steady inflow of related data—for example, on customer expectations and potential change orders, on impending price changes from suppliers, on how subcontractors are faring, and on how the rest of the business is doing.

All businesses run on data, of course. Trouble is, the data isn't always accurate. Somebody forgets to fill out a time sheet. Somebody else modifies a purchase order and never tells finance. If you have ever been through a full financial audit, you know that a company's books always contain a lot of errors. Most of the errors are small, even trivial—"not material," as the accountants put it—but often a few good-sized mistakes creep in. Our project management system is robust; large mistakes are likely to show up, just because you're watching the trend lines every week, and so you can correct them. But if the mistakes are too frequent, they will undermine the system's effectiveness. You need to be sure that data flows smoothly, and that it is accurate and as up to date as it can possibly be.

Of course, accuracy and timeliness aren't the only important factors. Two others are clarity and simplicity.

If you are an engineer or an accountant, you are accustomed to poring over complex databases and inspecting detailed spreadsheets. You won't be intimidated by a solid wall of numbers, whether they're on paper or on a computer screen. In that, you are different from most human beings. Most people look at a dense collection of numbers and instantly tune out, figuring they'll never understand it, so there's no point even trying. That's why Setpoint went from a "scoreboard" in the form of a printed spreadsheet to a scoreboard in the form of a big, hand-lettered whiteboard. People seem to find big, handwritten numbers easier to take in and discuss than tiny figures on a computer printout.

The more you can simplify what's on the scoreboard, the better. Even if it's simplified, though, the board won't solve the problem of numbers phobia. Let people get accustomed to the numbers gradually. Concentrate on just a few at a time. Explain what they mean, and don't hesitate to repeat yourself. Answer questions, and expect to answer the same question more than once. By the way, be absolutely sure that *you* understand what the numbers are saying before you get in front of your team to present them. Nothing will damage your credibility faster than having someone ask a *why* question that you can't answer.

Third: Make It "The Way We Do Things Around Here"

A company's culture, so it is said, defines what people do when no one is looking. It is the whole set of beliefs, values, and unspoken expectations that influence how people act in the workplace. Cultures differ radically from one company to another. Some cultures are highly distinctive, others purely conventional. Some cultures are amazingly effective in creating a great workplace, while others are wholly dysfunctional.

If you work for a big company, you're probably already aware of the cultural expectations that influence how people behave on the job. It's "the way we do things around here." If you run your own shop, you yourself have most likely created your company's culture. The culture will reflect how you treat people and what you expect from them. It will reflect how you define the company's priorities and ways of doing business. It will reflect your ethics and values.

The Project Management for Profit system is based on some fundamental cultural beliefs. People should hold themselves accountable for their performance. Most people work best when they "know the score"—when they understand how well they are doing and why. Project teams collaborate most effectively when everyone is on the same page, when everyone communicates openly and listens carefully, and when people treat one another with mutual respect. The system will fit most easily in companies where those values are already part of the culture—which, we like to think, includes most businesses. There are a few dictatorial companies, with "my way or the highway" and "we don't pay you to think" and "every two weeks we are even" cultures, that might not offer a receptive home to this system. But most companies will find that it works for them.

There's one thing that's essential, however, whatever your company's culture. The system needs to become a part of it— a given, an intrinsic element of the way you do things around here. You need to establish a rigorous discipline around compiling, analyzing, and discussing the data. You can't skip meetings, and you can't allow any of the boxes on the whiteboard to go unfilled.

We can't emphasize this point strongly enough: the easiest way to fail at Project Management for Profit is not to take it seriously. Heaven knows, many people have done just that; Dave of Quantum Robotics, whose story we told in chapter 8, is only one example. Sometimes it seems easier not to run the numbers. It's a busy week. Or it's a slow week. Or maybe you're just dreading a bad week. But you must continue to monitor and report the metrics on a regular basis. It will never become part of the culture if you do it only sporadically and halfheartedly. Keep the discipline of regular analysis and reporting alive and well!

With good implementation, we've found, the Project Management for Profit system carries benefits for all concerned.

If you're a business owner or senior executive, the system should give you the confidence that you really know how your projects and your overall business are faring. Most company owners rarely get this amount of data calculated and reported in a timely manner. Having all that information available to you, essentially on demand, is a surefire antidote to stress.

If you're a project manager, the system provides you with the tools and methodologies you need to monitor your project finances and guide your decisions in every phase of a project. It helps you identify profit-sucking problems and gives you the information you need to make course corrections in real time. Again: an antidote to stress.

If you're a participant on a project team, the system should give you confidence in the team's leaders. You know that you'll be getting accurate and timely feedback on the progress of your efforts and on the financial health of the venture. In this system, you're a key part of the team, and you will know the score as it's happening. If your stress levels aren't dropping yet, just give the system a chance. It won't disappoint you.

One last piece of advice: don't forget the magic word in the title of this book: *profit.* The game of business is all about making a profit. If a company can't earn a sustainable return, it won't survive. To be sure, there are a multitude of other great things that can happen in a business, and there are a lot of gauges and indicators that measure a business's success. But profit is like lift in aerodynamics: it keeps the aircraft in the air. If you don't have that, nothing else matters. Everything goes away if the business closes up.

Whether you're a business owner, a project manager, or a team member, your end goal has to be the same: to earn a long-term, sustainable profit on your work. To make the best possible decisions about profitability at every juncture of the project, you need to know what's going on *right now* with your project's financial performance. That, of course, is what this system and this book are about.

So we hope you will put the system to work. And we hope that, from now on, your projects will always come in on time and on budget—and that you will make some money while you're at it.

CHAPTER 12 TAKEAWAYS

- "Practice makes perfect." Good data, along with the discipline to present it every week to the team, will help make this system a part of your company's culture. Once it is part of the culture, your projects are more likely to come in on schedule and on budget.

- This stuff really works.

INDEX

ABOUT THE AUTHORS

Joe Knight is chief financial officer and co-owner of Setpoint, in Ogden, Utah, and co-owner and senior consultant with Los Angeles–based Financial Intelligence, Inc. He is coauthor of *Financial Intelligence* (Harvard Business School Press, 2006), *Financial Intelligence for Entrepreneurs*, *Financial Intelligence for HR Professionals*, and *Financial Intelligence for IT Professionals* (all Harvard Business School Press, 2008).

Roger Thomas's career includes twenty-seven years of successful project management experience in diverse fields, including amusement ride design, manufacturing, commercial construction, software engineering, computer hardware R&D, and custom automation systems.

Brad Angus is also a co-owner of Setpoint. A former management consultant with Ernst & Young, he has owned or managed several entrepreneurial businesses. He is coauthor of *The Fourth Dimension: The Next Level of Personal and Organizational Achievement* (John Wiley & Sons, 1996).